Start Your Business Right

"Get Start Your Business Right and accelerate your income with critical insights, tools and resources it takes most entrepreneurs years and thousands of dollars to discover. With this powerful success blueprint, you can begin creating the business and life you desire now."

— William R. Patterson, CEO, The Baron Solution Group

"Start Your Business Right takes us from thinking to doing to measuring achievements with the most comprehensive writing I have ever seen on the topic. It truly is a blueprint. Monica Davis, founder and publisher of *Exceptional People Magazine*, presents a clear, detailed, inspiring guidebook that anyone can pick up at any point in their life and elevate their results by following her advice. I highly recommend this book to anyone who wants more out of life."

— Jo Condrill, President, GoalMinds, Inc., and bestselling author of *101 Ways to Improve Your Communication Skills Instantly*

"Monica Davis has written a phenomenal book on business goals and ways to achieve them! I find this writing incredibly valuable and thorough! It's not just for those who have business goals in life, but also for people who need to establish goals for themselves. It is all encompassing and really is a must read for all! It is a great organizer and guide to promote a successful business and life!"

— Dean G. Campbell, President, Campbell Retirement Planning Centers, Inc.

"Start Your Business Right is an essential primer for any entrepreneur and business owner. Using probing questions that logically lead business owners to think more deeply about their business and personal missions and visions, Ms. Davis' book helps them chart a workable course for lasting success in both work and life."

— C.J. Scarlet, CEO and Chief Innovator, 10 for Humanity

Start Your Business Right

A Comprehensive Guide to Entrepreneurship Success

Second Edition

Monica Davis

An Atela Productions, Inc. Book

Copyright © 2020 by Monica Davis

Published in the United States of America by Atela Productions

Visit us on the web at https://www.secretstosuccessbooks.com

ISBN: 978-1-7348699-0-3

Ebook ISBN: 978-1-7348699-1-0

Library of Congress Control Number: 2013906980

Second Edition

Table of Contents

Preface

My goal in writing this book is to provide an important business planning resource for new entrepreneurs as well as seasoned business owners, CEOs, and professionals who want to achieve greater success at any level.

It is designed to give you an in-depth, analytical view into your overall business mission and the individual objectives required to accomplish the mission. The purpose of this book is to help you to analyze important aspects of your business so you can make solid decisions, effectively plan your objectives, and save time and money once you implement your business strategies. When you reduce the possibility of making mistakes early on, you increase your opportunity for maximum results much sooner.

After reading *Start Your Business Right*, you will have a much clearer understanding of your objectives, why you are starting your business, and how you can proceed successfully. You will also learn how to identify the most important resources for your business and create a solid plan to help eliminate costly mistakes before they happen.

Who Is This Book For?

If you answer "yes" to any one of these statements below, this book is for you.

- You're thinking of leaving the 9-to-5 work routine to become your own boss.

- You're a teenager with a desire to start a business or implement your bright idea and start the right way.

- You're retired but want to supplement your pension with additional income by starting a business.

- You're an innovator or inventor who wants to see a life-changing idea come to fruition.

- You've recently started a business but want to ensure you're building a solid foundation from the beginning.

- You've been in business for a few years but have realized important aspects of your business may not have been addressed early on and as a result, your venture is not as successful as it could be.

Start Your Business Right is intended to empower, inspire, and help you develop a blueprint for your business, no matter what level of experience you have as a business owner or entrepreneur. You can also use this as a guide to help you align your professional and business goals with your personal life so they are more balanced.

This book is designed to help you ask and answer the right questions and address important issues early on, which will set the foundation for success and enable you to make better decisions throughout the process.

Introduction

People are often quick to blame outside factors for slow business or lack of growth, but the hard truth is that your success does not depend on what's happening in the economy. Your success solely depends on you—your vision, your passion to succeed at whatever endeavor you choose, and your consistent actions towards your goals.

Start Your Business Right will help you discover ways to achieve greater success.

This book holds key information to support you as you thoroughly analyze your business and professional objectives, as well as blueprints you can use to create a working strategy for achieving your goals. What's on these pages will also help you uncover how to effectively approach and resolve business problems that you may encounter along the way.

If a house is going to withstand the test of time, it must be built from a blueprint or a plan that determines the integrity of its structure and results in a solid foundation. Everything that goes into building the house, from the materials to the workmanship, must involve integrity. You wouldn't expect a house built on a whim and cobbled together from cheap scrap materials to last very long or to provide a safe and sturdy place to make a home.

The same principle applies to everything you do in life.

If you want to operate a successful business, build a thriving career, or start a non-profit organization, you need to map out your strategy and develop a detailed plan. Ask yourself the following questions before jumping ahead:

- Are you building your company on a solid foundation?

- If you're starting a company, what's your plan?

- What things do you need to help you get to where you want to be?

- Who do you need to help you reach your goals and specific milestones?

This book serves as a guide to help you make smart decisions at the most detailed levels before and while you are creating your business; in other words, it will show you how to *Start Your Business Right*. You'll learn how to create a solid strategy as you work through the details of your vision, thereby enabling you to create the best path to success as an entrepreneur. It will also help you align your business goals with the rest of your life.

As you create your blueprint and build upon your foundation for both business and life, reinforce it with integrity and ethical plans of action. Yes, it may take a little longer and require more patience, but your rewards will be great. In whatever you do, I encourage you to design that same strong framework.

Also, included in this book are excerpts from individuals featured in *Exceptional People Magazine* (http://exceptionalmag.com). These snippets include great insights and business advice from exceptional people we've interviewed. Their backgrounds range from major corporate CEOs to marketing and financial gurus, and multi-millionaires and billionaires who developed their business empires from the ground up.

Not only will you gain exceptional insights, but you'll be inspired to reach well beyond your comfort zone to live your life to the fullest and create a business with unlimited potential.

Design Your Best Life

Each of us has been given a slate on which we can create our own masterpiece. This slate can become your blueprint for life. It is up to you to design your life and your business so that you have a foundation that can withstand obstacles and challenges that will come your way. A solid foundation will help you endure the rough times.

Your home was built from a blueprint or a plan that determined its structural integrity. Your life and your business must be built the same way. Design a blueprint for your business that will help you create or build unlimited opportunities supported by a foundation of integrity, ethical decisions, and plans of action.

This book provides you with a blueprint for designing your business and your life. Your business is an extension of who you are. Everything that you do in your business reflects on your beliefs and how you live your life. Make sure your blueprint is designed in a way that will leave a legacy of greatness and that others will want to follow. Go forth and design your masterpiece.

Make Mistakes, Innovate, and Understand the Void

My advice for small business owners, whether they have an online or offline business, is, first of all, don't be afraid to make mistakes. I'm sure I've made a countless number of mistakes. There is no such thing as starting a business and doing everything right, so making mistakes is part of the learning process.

Second, when you have an idea, make sure that it's an idea that is sustainable, and it gains you a competitive advantage in the marketplace. Make sure when you're starting up that you have a business model, a business model that includes a unique value proposition to your customer and understand why that would make you successful.

Most importantly, study your marketplace beforehand. Understand the void and try to address that rather than copying somebody else's idea and trying to be just another player in the marketplace.

I would say that if we just tried to merely become another Staples or Office Depot, we wouldn't be as successful. The fact that we sought to innovate, the fact that we offered so many green products, the fact that we are very much eco-friendly in terms of what we have to offer going forward to the future generations, is what makes us successful. When you look at the green movement, it's real and every single person has an obligation to leave the planet as good as they found it.

— Tony Ellison, Founder and CEO, Shoplet.com

Section One

Develop a Solid Plan for Life

The 7 Keys That Culminate in Success

There are several conditions necessary for achieving success and wealth. I think the first thing that is necessary would be a roadmap. And that roadmap can often come from a mentor, an advisor or a coach. I think that is the number one thing because there's no point in reinventing the wheel if someone has been there before you.

The second thing is what we would call your belief system—having a belief system that supports that idea of success. You have two different viewpoints of the world. You can view it from the point of scarcity, or you can view it from the point of abundance. It's very important for most people to take a viewpoint of abundance and possibility, as opposed to scarcity and lack.

That's one of the big differentiating factors that we found between our clients who achieve higher levels of success. They believe and they go into a situation believing that it's possible and that it will work, even if that belief, to some degree, may be unwarranted based on how they're going to do it.

Expanding your belief system is essential. One of the reasons that so many people struggle is they don't think big enough. I always tell people whatever dream that you have, make it ten times bigger than you're currently thinking because you'll attract more attention. You'll also attract a different type of people who are interested in what you are doing if you're operating in wider and bigger arenas.

The third thing that is necessary is your network and having the relationships that can get you to where you want to be, the relationships that can open a lot of doors. There's something that's called the Law of Significance that says nothing significant is ever accomplished alone.

We always talk about your network being a direct reflection of your net worth but when you look at this chain of six degrees of separation, that there's a chain of six people that separates everyone in the world from everyone else, it's essential that you start to build those relationships. You may be able to pick up a phone and call Bill Gates or Oprah, but the question is, have you built the relationship that would make them want to help you?

That's one of the big things, being able to cultivate your network.

The fourth thing is leveraging those vehicles, the proper vehicles for getting to your goal. If you're talking about financial success, then you're looking at real estate, the stock market, and entrepreneurship.

If you're talking about some other means of success, you really want to look at the vehicles that the most successful people have used to get to that goal, and you want to repeat that.

Knowledge and skills would be the fifth thing that you want to work on, continuing to read and learn. I always encourage people to continue to learn. If you don't like reading, there are lots of audio materials out there. There are video materials, but you should always continue to learn, upgrade your skills.

The sixth thing is the tools. Realize that there are a lot of great tools that will give you leverage and will provide you with more time so that you can accomplish more things. Investing in those tools can help you.

The last thing is taking action and doing the most important thing every day that will get you to your goal a lot faster. So, if your goal is to build a million-dollar business, you have to go after the million-dollar deals, or you have to go after enough small deals that can get you to a million dollars.

It's the culmination of those seven things: the mentor, the belief system, the network, choosing the right vehicles, the knowledge and skills, the tools and also taking the action, the most important action every day. Those are the things that I think become the culmination of success, as we've found in our research in working with so many different entrepreneurs.

— William R. Patterson,
Chairman and CEO of The Warcoffer Capital Group, LLC
Award-Winning Speaker, Business and Financial Expert

Go From Where You Are to Where You Want to Be

Your Attitude Counts

There are two things that will determine where you go in life, how far you will go, and whether you will achieve consistent success. Those two keys to success are your attitude and your actions. Are your circumstances keeping you from succeeding or is your attitude limiting your circumstances? Regardless of what your circumstances are, always remain in a positive frame of mind. Don't let what other people say and think about you determine your outcome.

The negative comments of others will block your success only if you let them. One of America's top motivational speakers, Les Brown, was inspired by one of his grade school teachers who told him, **"Someone's opinion of you doesn't have to become your reality."** What you say and think about yourself—not what others think or say—makes all the difference in the world.

Your outlook on life and what you think about yourself is a direct reflection of how you live your life. If you don't like the way your life has turned out or what it has developed into, review your outlook and begin to change it. Your outlook or perspective is the basis of your actions. We can expect the best from our lives, but ultimately what we put into it will determine what we get. Expect the best and use those expectations as the driving force to weave your destiny. The end results will be great achievements.

If you change your attitude about life, yourself, and those around you, you'll find there's a better way of living. If you maintain a positive attitude and react positively to every circumstance, even when situations are at their worst, you'll reap benefits and learn lessons that will last a lifetime.

What Does Success Mean to You?

Society has convinced us to believe that in order to become successful, you must make a lot of money and achieve material wealth. Before you can achieve success, you must know what it means to you. Most of us are successful and don't realize it. Success can mean doing something positive, excelling at what you do, or helping someone else succeed at something they desire. Success could also mean having a family that works and plays together, finishing what you start, and even enjoying what you do. The next time you get the feeling you're not successful, think about what you've done for others or that last project you completed or how you supported a friend who needed your moral support. Focus on the smaller things you have accomplished.

Achieving lifetime success is like building a home—you start from the bottom and you work your way up. You begin by laying the foundation, which consists of commitment, hard work, integrity, patience, and self-confidence. Then you add on more layers by building a team of people around who can help you achieve your dream. As you climb your way to the top, you know you're standing on a solid foundation.

Some of us may want to start directly at the top. When you choose that route, you might feel ill at ease. Without a strong foundation, you may be less prepared to handle the challenges you will encounter in life. If success for you means the following:

- **Attaining material things.** Identify those things that are important to you.

- **Establishing solid relationships.** Identify who those people are and how you will develop those relationships.

- **Helping others.** Identify those people and organizations you want to help and how you want to lend a helping hand.

Make a list of all the things you want to do. Review your list and prioritize the items beginning with the most important. Decide which goal you want to achieve first. This list can be the start of a new and brighter future for you and those around you.

Conquering Your Fears

Many people are afraid of trying something new or making changes in their lives. When you don't know what the end result is going to be, you become afraid to try something new. You may not be comfortable with your current circumstance, but at least you know what it is, and you are used to it.

Fear is a natural feeling, but it can keep you from experiencing many good things in life. When you let your fears guide you, you might miss out on new career opportunities, great relationships, or the opportunity to travel—all of which can enrich your life.

How do you overcome fear? Begin by acting on the very thing you are afraid of doing. Once you take action and combine those steps with confidence and faith, you'll be surprised how quickly your fears will disappear. Never be afraid to ask for help and go after what you want. Always approach your life with a positive attitude and integrity. Most importantly, don't be afraid of rejection. Approach your fears, setbacks, and disappointments with courage and determination. Soon you will find yourself becoming a stronger person each and every day.

Uncover Your Potential

Every person realizes his or her potential in a different way. Some people are self-motivated. They know what we want, they have dreams, they have a vision, and they immediately begin to act on it. They're always looking for ways to improve their lives, do something to improve the world, or impact the lives of others. They don't need to be told or reminded that they can achieve greatness. Some people are motivated by watching others succeed. Others are inspired by the things they are shown they can do, while other people have to hit rock bottom before they turn their lives around.

To reap the benefits of a fulfilling life, you must fully utilize your potential. Nurturing your potential is like planting a seed. You know that there's great potential for the plant to blossom and bloom, but there is a series of steps and actions that must occur before it grows. The seed must be nourished, watered, fertilized, and pruned as it grows. As you begin to utilize your full potential, you must nourish yourself with motivation, inspiration, and sometimes even desperation depending on your status in life. Surround yourself with people who seek excellence, have positive attitudes, keep a healthy outlook on life, and are self-motivated and successful. Learn from them, start thinking like them, and apply their methods for achieving success. You will begin to see a noticeable effect in every facet of your life. You will begin to experience the vast opportunities that await you.

Many years ago, when I started working as a secretary for a federal agency, I wasn't aware of my full potential and what impact I would have as an employee. I was always interested in technology, so I began to learn a lot of new things in my spare time as they were introduced to the market. I applied what I learned at work whenever possible. I discovered that my contributions had a huge impact on the way we did business.

What I didn't know was that my boss also realized my potential. He gave me the opportunity to broaden my experience beyond my wildest dreams by recommending me as a technology expert for a support team for the Secretary of the agency. By the age of 20, I was traveling around the world providing technological expertise to people who served the highest office in the agency. From that point on, I was motivated to continue to learn new things and to perform at my best at all times. Whatever you choose to do, be the best at it because you never know who is watching you or when your next great opportunity will strike.

Take Charge of Your Life

Sometimes, you might hear a person say, "I wonder why my life is so difficult?" or "I just can't seem to get ahead." Living is not difficult. It is the decisions we make as individuals and collectively as a human race that make living difficult. Investigate the choices you make, the people you surround yourself with, and from whom you take advice.

We must raise our expectations about our own abilities and then strive to meet them. We tend to blame others or society for our circumstances. If after a few years you haven't gotten that raise you feel you deserve, rather than complain about your boss year after year, create a plan of action, develop a blueprint for change, and then act on it. Don't wait for your boss to give you a raise. Create your own opportunities. Seek another position or start your own business. Place yourself in a position to achieve success.

Life is all about choices. Some people will make a decision they know is entirely inappropriate. But because the decision is easy and convenient, they make the choice because it gives them instant gratification. It speaks volumes about their values. Either they have not established the proper values or are not committed to the things that are important to them.

Don't change directions with the wind. Remain steadfast in your values. Take charge of your life by using the values you set for yourself and your company as a guide for making the best decisions for your life.

> *The secret of success is constancy to purpose.*
> — Benjamin Disraeli, British prime minister

Defining Your Personal Values

Before you can lead others, first you must know yourself. Many of us have an extraordinary ability to become great leaders. Leadership that comes from the heart will inspire others to follow.

You will find your core values within yourself. Some common values include loyalty, trust, and passion. Our core values define who we are. They drive and motivate us to act.

It is imperative that you remain true to your core values in your personal and work life. Once you establish the values that are most important to you, commit to them and live by them daily. Not only will others be willing to follow and stand by you, but also you will discover that you will have an amazing impact on your organization.

Know Your Worth and Stop Believing in Luck

The very first day in my class, I take a $20 bill out of my pocket and show it to the class. I ask, "If I were to give it to someone, who would want to take this twenty-dollar bill, no strings attached?"

Everyone raises their hand. The next thing I do is crumple it into a ball and throw in the trash can.

Then I ask, "Now, who still wants that twenty-dollar bill?"

Everyone, of course, still raised their hand.

I said to them, "That shows you that you have worth. No matter what you've been told, or no matter what your situation is, or if someone told you that you couldn't accomplish something, you must think of yourself as that twenty-dollar bill, whether it's a crisp new bill in a new leather wallet, or if it's crumpled in the trash can. If you unfold it, you don't have to iron it to make it look new again. If you take it to the bank, they will accept it. That's how you should think about your lives."

The second thing I tell them is, "There's no such thing as luck. You know what luck is? Luck is when opportunity meets preparation or vice versa. If you prepare yourself and opportunity knocks, then you can walk through the door."

Some people walk through without preparation, and that's why they don't succeed.

— Kermit Griffin, Culinary Historian,
One of America's Top Cultural Chefs

Identify and Set Goals That Work for You

People who enjoy what they do are usually more successful than those who are not enlightened by their daily experiences. A goal can be anything that is important, meaningful, or will enhance your life in some way. When you set goals for yourself and work to achieve them, you are paving a road to creating a better life for you and those around you. Everything that you do can potentially result in a ripple effect. Make sure your daily actions have a positive effect on the people who surround you.

The best way to accomplish goals is to write them down and constantly keep them in front of you. A good way to identify and set realistic goals is to make note of the things you're good at, enjoy doing, want to acquire, or want to achieve. This is an opportunity to identify your talents, create a plan to pursue them, and take them to their limits. For example:

If you...	You may want to...
Get along well with people	Pursue a career in public relations
Work well with numbers	Be a bookkeeper or an accountant
Like working with plants	Open a flower shop
Enjoy cooking	Be a chef, caterer, or restaurateur
Enjoy writing	Become an independent writer
Are a natural leader	Pursue a career as a manager
Have excellent math skills	Develop a career as an engineer

Here are some ideas and questions that you can ask yourself to help you start creating your goals:

- What would you like to become?

- What skills would you like to master?

- What are your career goals?

- What are your personal goals?

- Do you want to be an entrepreneur? If so, what type of business do you want to create?

- What characteristics would like to have?

- What fears would you like to conquer?

- What kind of relationships do you want to develop?

  What types of relationships are important you?

  With whom do you want to make connections?

  How can you improve or change your current relationships?

- What new things would you like to learn?

- What are your spiritual or intellectual goals?

- How would you like to help your community?

- What are your goals for your personal values?

- What are your social and recreational goals?

  Do you want to attend a variety of games and concerts?

  Do you want to travel? If so, where?

- What are your financial goals?

  How much money do you want to make annually? Weekly? Monthly?

  What is your ideal net worth?

  What are your investment goals (e.g., IRAs, real estate, mutual funds)?

  How much do you want to contribute to charity?

- How much money do you want to invest for your child's future?

- What are your material goals?

  Do you want to own a home? If so, where do you want to live? What kind of home do you want? What options are most important to you?

Do you want to own a new car? If so, what type, style, color, and options are important to you?

When setting goals, you must be specific in terms of what you wish to accomplish. You should set goals that are reasonable and create realistic timelines for achieving them. Set goals that you are confident you can obtain. Start by setting short-term goals and then aim for intermediate and long-term goals.

Your goals must be:

Achievable: Setting goals that are unachievable defeats your purpose and your vision. Do you have the confidence, resources, and stamina to achieve your goals?

Specific: Without specificity how will you know when you have accomplished or achieved your goals? Your goals must be clearly defined.

Measurable: How will you measure your success? What results do you want to achieve? Are you meeting the needs of the people you are serving?

Results-driven: What is the result you want to achieve? What outcome do you want to achieve from your goal?

Detailed-oriented: You should have a clear outline for your company's goals. You and your colleagues should have a plan that will help you understand how to go from point A to point B and beyond.

Time-sensitive: Goals without specific times of completion are just dreams. For every goal you set, you must also establish a timeline by which you will complete it.

Examples of Professional and Personal Goals

Professional Goals

- Sell one million gadgets by next March.

- Earn an MBA within the next four years.

- Obtain a supervisory position in the next year.

- Become a member of the Board of Directors for the organization of my choice within the next six months.

- Arrive on time to work every day.

- Take three professional development courses in the next quarter.

Personal Goals

- Learn how to play pinochle before the next game.

- Have three children by age 30.

- Purchase a sports car by the end of the year.

- Plan a trip to the Bahamas for next summer.

- Quit smoking in six months.

- Plan a romantic walk with my spouse every Friday night.

Whether your goals are professional or personal, effective goal setting requires you to do the following:

- State what you want to do with your goals by making them well defined and realistic.

- Have a general idea of what it will take to achieve your goal by performing an analysis.

- State how and when you're going to achieve your goal by establishing a realistic timeframe and creating an action plan.

- Take actions that are consistent with achieving your goals.

Self-improvement is a lifelong endeavor. No rule says you must be excellent in all things or master everything that you do. Find that one thing you're good at and take it to the limit. The minute you get that one good idea, start working on it. Write down your thoughts as they come to you. All your goals don't have to be long term, complicated, or extremely involved. You can set smaller, more straightforward goals first. The bottom line is to identify, pursue, and complete them. Sometimes your goals will require you to get help from others.

If you need other people to help you achieve your goals, seek individuals who are ambitious and want to help you. Build a team that will work for you and with you. Your team should include individuals who have the following characteristics:

- Believe in themselves and their own abilities to succeed

- Support you and your vision

- Are self-motivated

- Are committed to excellence

Leisure, some degree of it, is necessary to the health of every man's spirit. — Harriet Martineau

Maintain Your Enthusiasm

Revive Yourself

Starting and running a business is a serious endeavor. To maintain your enthusiasm, periodically reward yourself as you accomplish major steps and overcome difficult obstacles. Fulfilling your business goals should be an exciting challenge. To re-energize yourself, sometimes you need to separate yourself from the things you are most determined to achieve. Knowing when to take a break is just as important as achieving the goal itself.

Here are a few ideas on how to unwind and re-energize:

- Take a walk.
- Meditate.
- Treat yourself to something nice or exciting.
- Go out to dinner.
- Do absolutely nothing for a few hours.
- Listen to your favorite music.
- Volunteer to do something for someone else.
- Do something daring such as skydiving.

For executives, managers, and businesses owners, reward your employees for their dedication and loyalty in these ways:

- Treat them to lunch.
- Do something special for their birthday.
- Give a talented employee a raise or certificate of appreciation.
- Give your staff members a day off.
- Treat your employees to a special occasion for a job well done.

Assess Your Accomplishments

Take Time to Reflect Upon Your Achievements

Whether you accomplish your business tasks or personal goals on a daily, weekly, or monthly basis, creating a habit of reviewing them after completion will help you improve over time. The more time it takes to complete your goals, the more often you should review your progress. Take time to reflect upon prior experiences from a positive point of view.

When you assess your accomplishments, ask yourself the following questions to help you plan better for the future:

- Could I have been more prepared for the task or goal?

- What can I do to improve this task for the next time? For example, if you are teaching a course, prepare a feedback questionnaire for your participants to complete. Analyze the responses and determine what areas need to be enhanced or modified. Use the survey to improve the next course.

- Can I apply some of the same principles to my next task or goal?

- What steps can I eliminate or add to improve the overall process?

- What can I do to avoid certain pitfalls?

One important thing to do is compliment yourself for starting and completing your goals because it takes commitment, endurance, and courage, especially when the path to success becomes burdened with obstacles.

Section Two

Develop a Solid Plan for Your Business

An Entrepreneur Has a Realistic Plan, Not a Dream

It's one thing to have a great idea, but you have to be pragmatic about it, too. It's one thing to have dreams, but you can't be unrealistic about your dreams. There's a difference between having a dream and having a realistic plan because that's what being an entrepreneur is.

It's being able to have a plan to make that dream into some sort of reality. You have to be able to say, "How do I get from point A to point B?" Not just, "Gee, I'd love to be at point B."

How do I market it? How do I finance it? What about all these other elements including people and skills—where are they coming from? Do I have them? Does someone else have them? Do I have to buy them? Can I have them as a partner?

That's what the mindset has to be. "Yes, it's a great dream and I have a vision," but you also have to be able to put that into a pragmatic set of procedures and steps, so you can get from point A to point B.

Some of the common mistakes new entrepreneurs make—the two most obvious things that affect almost everybody—is management and money. Management in terms of having the right skill set.

You have to be able to approach a market, to approach a product, or approach a manufacturing process with enough experience or knowledge to make that happen. On the money side, it's not only having enough money, it's being able to project a reasonable amount of money you're going to need and not being so anxious. This is one of the mistakes I made.

Sometimes you can become so anxious and eager, you start to do things that you probably shouldn't do. For example, if you project that you need X dollars and someone says to you, "I'll give you part of X now, and I'll give you part of X later," and then you say "Oh, boy. I've got the commitment for the money I need," but you know what? There's timing to cash flow.

There is a value to cash, and just because someone says they're going to give you that total amount of money, the way you run a business isn't necessarily consistent with the way they want to do it. If you need to buy inventory today, so you can sell it and generate revenues and all of a sudden you have to spend that money on rent then, when that person gives you the rest of money, they say, "Well, where's the profit you said we'd generate?"

You may say, "Well, you didn't give me enough to buy the product. You only gave me enough to pay the rent." And then everybody's unhappy. Does it mean you have to be skeptical and not trust anyone? That's a tough way to run a business and a tough way to go through life if you can't trust anybody.

Planning is also very important. It's realistic planning. It's not just saying, "I can make this for a dollar and sell it for two dollars."

The question is, "When do you have to pay that dollar? When do you get the two dollars?" That has to do with detailed planning of what are you going to have to spend, and when are you are going to have to spend it. That cash flow projection is critical to understanding the business.

— Jeff Stoller, Jeff Stoller Associates,
Financial and Legal Consultant

A Prelude to Business Success

Set Yourself Up for Success in Your Business

There are many ways you can achieve goals faster and more effectively. The following section includes an in-depth roadmap to help you plan and execute your goals. Using these tools will help you execute your goals quickly and plan for potential challenges you may encounter along the way. Any entrepreneur, CEO, or executive can use this guide to identify the best way to achieve specific goals and overcome business challenges.

Define and Communicate Your Company's Goals

Have you defined your company's goals? What's the big picture? What individual goals or tasks will make up the big picture? Until you have a clear picture of your company's goals or its purpose, neither you nor your employees will understand the company's mission. Your staff won't feel like they're an important part of the team, and they won't understand their purpose or roles.

As a business owner, you must communicate your company's goals to your employees. Each employee needs to have a clear understanding of where you are, the state of the company, and how he or she can help you get there. You need to create a process where EVERY employee understands your goals and how his or her individual goals are aligned with your vision and mission.

Analyze Your Goals and Objectives

Once you have identified your business goal or idea, you're ready to create a plan that will guide you as you execute your idea. Thorough planning is a necessity in executing any long-term goal. This is especially important if you want to succeed as a business owner. Take time to fully analyze your business goals, your purpose, your mission, and your plan for running your business.

Analyze Your Business Goals

Analyzing your business goals and objectives allows you to carefully plan ahead to avoid costly mistakes that can delay or hamper your success as you build your business. Performing a goal analysis will help you to achieve the following objectives:

- Define your purpose.

- Think about how your goal will affect your life, your family, and other important people in your immediate circle.

- Identify short-term and long-term benefits and obstacles.

- Create a detailed overview and understanding about running your business and achieving your specific goals.

Determine if the results will be worth your effort. For example, do you believe you will receive the return on investment that you expect?

The Philosophy of Will, Skill, and Refill

Our country needs entrepreneurs and small business owners more than ever. Big business is not going to rescue this nation. It's going to be small business owners and entrepreneurs getting better in growing and hiring and doing what they do best. It's always been that way.

If you're an entrepreneur or small businessperson, what an awesome place to be but you've got a huge responsibility.

You owe it to yourself and your family and everyone to do the right things in order to get there. That's where you practice the will, skill, and refill philosophy where you're filling your mind with the right things so you can have the right attitude, the right motivation, and the right desire and you're learning the right things to enhance and grow your business, whether that's marketing, sales, or how to manage your budget.

If you want to be successful at something, if you want your training program to take you to the next level, or on a personal level you want to go to the next level, then you've got to have these three things.

Will is simply the heart, the desire, the passion, the motivation, and the attitude to get it done, the belief that you can get it done.

Skill is the how-to, the process, and the technique. It's the hard learning, the experience, and expertise.

The refill means you have to do it every day. You have to work on the will and skill every day.

You owe it to yourself to understand how to have a successful business in all the areas that are important, like sales, marketing, budgeting, product development, and operations. Take inventory to see what you're good at and not good at. Obtain the skills in the areas that you need improvement in.

— Tom Ziglar, CEO, Zig Ziglar Corporation

Recognizing the Components for Your Goals

Analyzing your business goals can also help you avoid or prepare for possible pitfalls along the way. All goals will involve three or more of the following factors:

- Purpose
- Skills
- Time
- Education
- Materials
- People
- Potential problems
- Marketing
- Advertising
- Budget
- Return on investment (ROI)

Defining Your Purpose

As you begin analyzing your goals, use the following questions to help you discover your purpose.

Purpose and Vision

- Why do I want to achieve this goal? What is my vision or mission for the company?

- Why am I committed to the business? Am I in this to enhance my social life or professional skills? Do I want to be in this business to provide a better life for me and my family? Can I offer something positive to society?

- How will this business affect my life in the short and the long run? What changes or adjustments will I have to make in my personal or professional life?

- How can I use this goal to enhance my personal or professional life? Can I use my earnings to travel the world and learn about other cultures?

- What will happen if I don't achieve my goal? How will I feel if I don't achieve my desired result?

- Will the results be worth my effort?

- Does my family, spouse, or significant other completely support my decision to start and run a business?

- After I have completed my goal, what will I do next?

- Will my business be a full-time endeavor, or will it be a part-time opportunity?

- Will I remain the sole proprietor or will I bring on employees or partners?

- If I am in the beginning stages of my business, have I researched and considered the pros and cons of the different business structures, such as sole proprietorship, LLC, C corporation, or S corporation?

Products and Services

- What product(s) or service(s) will I provide?

- Who are my competitors?

- Have I done the research on my competitors?

- What can I offer that is different or unique? What is my unique selling proposition (USP)?

- How will my potential customers or clients benefit from my products or services?

Taking an Inventory of Your Skills

What skills will you need to run your business? Begin thinking about your skills as you consider the following questions:

- Do I need special skills to run the business?

- What current skills do I already have that can be applied to the business?

- Do I need to develop my existing skills?

- What additional skills do I need?

- How much will it cost?

- How long will it take to develop these skills?

- Where will I obtain the necessary skills? On the job? At a special trade school? With additional training? Or, can I teach myself?

- Where will the funds come from? Can I use my personal funds? Will I need loans? Can I borrow from friends and family? Will I need to work overtime or get a second job?

Evaluating Your Educational Background

Recognizing your educational skills and limitations is critical to your business success. Ask yourself the following questions:

- Do I have the enough education to proceed?

- Do I have the right kind of education? What type of education do I need?

- Can I complete my course work in the timeframe that I have set for achieving my business goals?

- Who will fund my education? Can I pay for my own education? Can I get a bank loan? Can I get a college loan? Does my company have a tuition reimbursement program?

- Where will I obtain my education? Will I attend a traditional college or an online institution?

- How far and how often will I have to travel for my education? Will there be a daily, weekly, or monthly schedule?

- How will my educational pursuits affect my time, my family's time, and my other responsibilities?

Mapping Out Your Time

Many business owners underestimate how much time it will take to develop a successful business. Get an accurate pulse of your time by looking at the following factors:

- How much time will I have to commit to achieve my business or professional goal?

- Am I willing to consistently devote my time and energy to my goals?

- Have you asked yourself the following questions about your time?

Should I achieve my goal at a pace that is conducive to my current lifestyle?

Should I change my lifestyle to accommodate my business?

Should I make my business goals a higher priority in my life?

Can I work on this goal in addition to my other priorities?

Can I maintain my same level of efficiency?

How will this goal affect my time, my family's time, and my other commitments?

- Should I quit my job to pursue my entrepreneurial dream?

- Have you asked yourself the following questions about your day job?

Can I financially afford to quit my job now?

Do I want to take a high risk and quit anyway?

Can I work my regular job and run the business at the same time?

How long should I work for my employer and pursue my business goals simultaneously?

Will focusing on my business diminish the quantity and quality of my productivity at work?

Can I adjust my work schedule to spend more time on my business?

What other setbacks could I encounter?

The Most Successful Businesses Are Built on Passion

My best advice for anyone who wants to start a business—male or female—is honing in on your passion. Figure out what makes you tick, what you enjoy doing, what you're good at, and go from there.

Don't necessarily look at other people and say, "Oh, they're making so much money doing this," or "Look how successful somebody is doing that."

If the business doesn't fit your skill set and what you love to do, you'll never succeed. You should go to work every day doing something that you love, and things will grow from there.

You have to look at yourself and say, "What am I good at, and where do I fall short?" Use that information to build a realistic business. If you're not a people person, then plan to be the back end, but outsource that skill to somebody else. Go in with realistic expectations of what you're good at and what you're not good at doing.

— Debra Cohen, President, Home Remedies of NY,
Creator, Homeowner Referral Network (HRN)

Making the Most of Your Materials

Will you have all the materials you need to make your business work? Consider the following questions:

- What materials or equipment will you need?

- How much will you need to achieve your goal?

- How often will you need to purchase these materials?

- How much will the materials cost?

- If you don't have enough money, can you trade or barter with another company?

- Who will provide your materials? Who will be your vendors? Where are they located?

- How will you pay for your materials? Will you need a business loan? Can you borrow money from family or friends?

- Should you invest in insurance coverage for the business?

- Will you need any additional technology to run your business?

  If so, do you already know how to use them efficiently enough to get the job done?

  If not, how much time will it take you to learn these new applications well enough to get the job done?

- Should you hire someone to handle any work that requires specific skills outside of your expertise?

Gauging How Your Goals Will Affect the People in Your Life

Your business may soar, but how will your friends and loved ones be affected? Think about the following criteria as you develop your plans:

Family and Friends

- Who else may be affected while you are in the process of starting and running your business or working toward your goal (e.g., family or friends)? Will you need them to step in and help?

- How will they be affected in the short and long term? Will they have to take off from work, give up personal time, or create space for you?

- Will your friends and family members have to take over your obligations?

- Will they need to make sacrifices for you?

Business and Moral Support

- What individuals can you rely on as mentors, leaders, and motivators to help you stay on course, effectively run your business, or complete your goal?

- Who will you need to help you run your business or accomplish your goal?

- What type of people will you need? Will you need people with special skills or knowledge, connections with social or business organizations, access to financial institutions?

- Where are these people or organizations located?

- Where and how will you find them?

- When are they available?

- What are their fees?

- What will they expect from you in return?

- How much time are they willing to commit to you?

- What is the quality of their work ethic?

Payment for Support Provided

- If you don't have the money to pay them for their services or products, what can you offer in exchange?

- Could you ask friends, associates, or family members to help you implement certain tasks for free?

- If so, what can you offer in return? Can you pay them later when the business is financially stable? Can you offer them a small portion or a percentage of your profits?

Commitment of Other Supporters

- Do they have the relevant skills or experience to do the work?

- Are they 100% committed to helping you?

- Can you count on these people to provide quality work without pay?

- Will they make your work a priority?

- How long should you ask for pro bono work from family or friends before you hire an expert?

Exploring All of Your Options

Have you thought about every single thing you can do to make your business a success? Consider the following list as you think about all your options:

- Should you do most or all the work if you don't have the funds?

- Will you have the time to perform every task of the business until you can afford to hire other people?

- Have you identified all the processes that need to be in place to run your business well?

- How will taking on the lion's share of the work affect your other obligations?

- Have you created a plan for bringing on part-time or full-time employees?

  If so, do you have the proper structure in place for hiring employees (e.g., medical and insurance benefits, payroll taxes, job descriptions)?

If not, can you hire freelancers, contractors, or other vendors to handle these tasks?

- Do you have an attorney who can assist you with any legal issues that may arise with your employees?

- Do you have an accountant who can help you with payroll, taxes, and other accounting procedures?

- Can you hire a virtual assistant for your administrative tasks?

- Can you hire interns? If so, do you have access to nearby colleges and universities with excellent intern programs? What roles can they fill in your business? Will you have time to train them?

- Who should you network with to encourage business growth, partnerships, and joint ventures?

- Which organizations should you join that will boost your business?

Business Is Confusing If You Don't Have Your Tribe

There are a lot of confusing things in business. The best way to demystify them, whether it's marketing or getting better cash flow in your business, is to look at who is in your tribe, who your personal advisors are.

You need to build a community of trusted advisors so when you have opportunities to grow your business, but you're not informed or educated enough, you have people to help demystify them for you.

— Jodie Shaw, Chief Marketing Officer,
The Alternative Board, United Kingdom

A Successful Business Needs a Good Team and Smart Research

One of the key things to starting a business is assembling a good team. Whether it's a team of people to work with or a team of people to advise and support you. I was very lucky with my London Business School associates and a few other people I involved in the business. Although I was running it myself, I was able to pick up the phone and get advice and help from them. Without it, the business wouldn't be where it is today.

I would say don't get put off but make sure that any new business you think of going into is well-researched. I think people dive into things without really understanding the market and the players and competitors. I did a lot of competitive analysis before I started, so I knew exactly what I was up against, what other companies were charging. I researched everything about the car and taxi market in London. I think those are the key things to do. Make sure the planning process is well done. If you miss something, the business can be completely and fundamentally flawed.

— Nicko Williams, Founder, Climatecars, United Kingdom

Creating Your Team

The people you select to support your business, professional, and personal goals should be loyal to your vision and mission. Your team members should have the following characteristics:

- Timely
- Trustworthy and honest
- Believe in themselves and their abilities to succeed
- Believe in you, your vision, and your dreams
- Take risks to meet their goals
- Open to new ideas
- Willing to help you achieve your goal
- Able to admit mistakes and learn from them
- Willing to apologize when they are wrong
- Can work as part of a team
- Self-motivated
- Committed to excellence and enhancing their lives
- Will provide positive feedback on your performance

Facing Potential Challenges

Every business must face hard times. Will you be prepared? Think about the following questions as you create your business plan:

- What difficult challenges and obstacles might you have to overcome?
- Have you created a list of possible challenges and solutions (e.g., unforeseen illness in the family, new expenses for your children, a key employee leaves, a competitor has developed a better product)?
- Have you made plans for the worst-case scenarios?

- What resources might you need to overcome challenges?

- Who can you rely on to help you with potential challenges (e.g., support groups, family, professional support)?

  How long will you need them to help you?

  Will they expect to be paid?

  How much and how often?

- How much could it cost you to fix this challenge or problem? What if you don't have enough funds?

- Can you afford to push the problem aside until you can afford to pay someone?

- Will this affect your business, employees, and partners?

- Can you reallocate your funding to take care of the problem?

- Will reallocating your funding affect your payroll, vendors, and other people who support your business? If so, how quickly can you replenish your funds?

- Are you willing to invest the time to fix any potential problems?

- Will focusing on a potential problem take time away from your business or your employees?

- Will your employees or business partners be willing to devote the time and resources to helping you solve your challenges?

Creating a Marketing and Advertising Strategy

How will you get the word out about your business? Use the following questions to help you think about promoting your business:

- Who will be the target market for your product (e.g., auto purchasers, entrepreneurs, hospitals)?

- Who is in this demographic? What are their ages, marital status, income level, educational level, and gender?

- Where are they located?

- How will you reach them (e.g., telemarketing, direct mail, TV, newspaper ads, word of mouth, press releases, social media networking)?

- How will customers purchase your products or services?

- How much money are you willing to spend on marketing? How will you cover your marketing expenses?

- What kind of image or brand do you want to create?

- How will you attract potential customers?

- What is your message? How will you say it?

- What about the psychographics of your customers—their thoughts, feelings, opinions, values, and attitudes?

Does Your Content Marketing Have Value?

The biggest mistake that everybody makes—both large companies and entrepreneurs—is being too in love with their own brand. Much of the product and marketing material I see is written for the person who already loves that business or product: "Here is why we are so awesome."

What that message needs to do, however, is show what that company knows about you. Mr. Prospect: "Here are the ways this item can make your life better."

Whether you're a small, mid-sized, or large company, selling to businesses or selling to consumers, your customers are going to connect with you because you are helping them solve a problem or improve their quality of life. It's basic psychology. When you can make people understand why your product or service will enable them to have a better result, you've got a much better chance of being successful.

Some people may say content marketing is the best way to fuel brand awareness. Every communication that a company releases is a piece of marketing. If your sales lead is having a conversation with a prospect, or if someone's sends an email, it's all marketing. Each communication is a piece of valuable content representing the company brand.

Content marketing today is the strategic use of all these moments where we interact with prospects and clients. I believe content marketing is extremely valuable. When leveraged appropriately, it is no longer just another ad on a web page or Facebook feed. Instead, you become a trusted piece of referred content that people receive from someone they know—who knows them and understands them, their likes and dislikes. That comes with much more credibility.

Content marketing requires a significant investment of time and a different way of thinking. Everything we do all day, every day, is content marketing. It's a matter of harnessing it and distributing it strategically online.

> — Jeanniey Mullen, Award-Winning Marketing Expert,
> Chief Marketing Officer, DailyPay

Balancing Your Budget

How much money will you need? Will you need help organizing your finances? Use the following steps to begin developing a plan for keeping your finances on point:

- How much money will you need to begin and continue your business plan?

- What is your three- and five-year plan?

- Where will you get your funding?

- Will you need an accounting system to set up your business?

Borrowing from Your 401K

- Can you use your 401K to fund your business at the beginning?

- If so, how will this affect your individual finances?

- When will you replenish your funds?

- Can you have the repayment withdrawn from your paycheck?

- Will you have to pay any penalties?

Borrowing Other Money

- Are you willing to take out a loan?

- If so, when?

- How much are you willing to take out?

- Who will you borrow from?

- What will be the purpose of the loan (e.g., to cover specific materials, trainings, overhead)?

- What if you spend more than you anticipate? Where will the additional funds come from?

- Do you have enough money set aside for personal and business emergencies?

- When should you begin paying yourself a salary?

- Will you need to open a separate business account?

- What are the requirements for opening a business bank account in my state?

Taking Out a Line of Credit

- Will you need to open a line of credit for your business?

  If so, how will this affect your overall credit score?

  Will you need to open more than one line of credit?

- What is your debt-to-income ratio?

- Should you anticipate being denied a line of credit?

- How will these denials affect your overall credit rating?

- Have you researched the best interest rates?

- Will you be able to consistently make your payments to avoid late fees and higher interest rates?

Other Funding Sources

- Do you qualify for any grants or fundraising efforts?

- Will you use crowdfunding as a source for starting your business or for developing a new product?

Planning for a Return on Investment (ROI)

Will this business venture be worth your time and investment? Ask yourself the following questions to ensure that you will get a sufficient ROI:

- What results do you want from your business?

- How will you feel once you've met certain goals or milestones?

- Do you want your end results to be financial, material, or emotional?

  Will accomplishing this goal make you feel better as a person?

Will it allow you to purchase a new home?

Will it allow you to drastically increase your annual income?

Will it allow you to serve your community and give back to others?

- What new products or services can you develop to increase your ROI?

- Are you happy with your current ROI? If not, what is keeping you from getting a higher level of return?

- What areas of your business do you need to change to achieve maximum results?

Learn to Master the Art of Sales

When you are communicating with a prospect on the telephone, you can listen for specific things that indicate whether the person has the intention to buy. You can listen to their tone, pacing, words, energy level, volume level, and syntax.

All of that is critical when you are communicating over the phone. I deal with many clients who do most of their work on the telephone. You can hear when someone is drifting. You don't have to see them. You don't have to have someone sitting in front of you to hear that they are disconnected from the conversation.

If your personality has what I call the "magnet appeal," then you can learn a system for selling as well as the psychology behind it.

> — Linda Clemons, Global Speaker and Expert
> Sales and Nonverbal Communications

You Won't Have Anything If You Don't Take Care of Your Customers

If your customers are telling you what they want, you need to listen to them. If your customers have a problem with something, you treat that product like it's your very own. With our customer service, we don't let people go to recordings. We answer the phone every time. We pride ourselves on it.

I don't answer the phone very often, but if anybody ever wants to talk to me, they're more than welcome. I give them my direct line. Customer service—our customers built our company. If we don't take care of them, what do we have? Our customers are our best salespeople.

The question becomes, how long do you want to be in business? Do you want to be in business for two years, or do you want to stay in business and be able to pass it down to your family?

— Rich van Engers, President, Sturdi Products, Inc.

Create an Action Plan for Your Business

A plan of action is a list of specific actions you intend to take to achieve your goal. The action plan is usually a document that states what you're going to do and how you're going accomplish it. It is a road map that gives you direction as you begin to move forward. Your action plan allows you to track your progress. You should use your action plan to accomplish the following:

- **Break** your business goals into smaller, manageable steps.

- **Prioritize** your objectives.

- **Set timelines** for your start date, intended completion date, and actual completion date.

- **List specific actions** or steps you intend to take to achieve your business goals.

- **List of pros and cons** to help you focus on the individual components of the business.

- **Review** your progress.

You can have a mental plan or a written plan of action. A written plan is always better because it allows you to track your progress and map out your success. Mental plans of action can be used for very short and specific goals.

A mistake business owners often make is looking at the whole picture and becoming overwhelmed by the amount of work and details involved. Achieving goals are like puzzles. You must complete them piece by piece. Set a reasonable time frame for achieving each part. As you progress, review your plan often to determine where you are and where you should be based on your timetable. After you complete one step, move on to the next without hesitation or procrastination. Do not get into the habit of setting unrealistic goals or setting unreasonable timelines. Some goals look easy on paper, but they often take more time than you might realize.

Don't take on too many objectives or goals at one time. Create a pace that is conducive for your lifestyle. Each time you don't meet your timelines or objectives, your motivation may begin to diminish. You may even lose interest or confidence in your ability to achieve your goals. So set a pace that works for you.

For example, today is Tuesday and your boss tells you that he wants a report along with supporting figures and documents on his desk by Friday afternoon. You now have four days to decide what tasks need to be accomplished each day and in what order they should be completed.

Why not establish a similar process to achieve your business goals? Make notes and follow through on them. If necessary, place your goals and your action plan in the location where you spend most of your time. Do whatever you need to do to ensure that you complete your goals.

Consistency is key to achieving success. Even if you don't have a lot of time to devote to your business in the beginning, just do one thing every day towards accomplishing your business objectives. Instead of watching television for an hour, take 20 minutes to work on your goal. You'll be amazed at what you will accomplish in a short period of time and how much closer you will be towards achieving your dreams.

As an entrepreneur or business owner, you must be willing to endure the challenges that will you encounter. You're not running a race. You must proceed at a pace that is appropriate for you and the people in your life. Don't compare yourself to others or how quickly they are achieving success in their lives. It is a natural feeling to sometimes want to keep up with others. But remember that success is unique to each individual. What you accomplish is based on your passion, determination, capabilities, and the people with whom you surround yourself.

In an earlier book, *On the Receiving End: A Collection of Works for Realizing the Potential Within*, I wrote the following poem:

Endurance

by Monica Davis

Endurance. A test of faith, a test of strength.
As you travel through this journey called life,
your trials and tribulations may be many.
When the hills you climb seem steeper and longer,
Just hold on to your faith and your strength
and your passion to continue will become stronger.

Sometimes life is like a door.
As you begin to open it,
There are hidden obstacles on the other side
that may block your vision.

Endurance is what you must have.
The obstacles become a test of your strength and determination.
Don't let the adversities of life keep you out.
Endure—they're not everlasting.

Life is sometimes like a race.
Some will pass you by and
others will fall behind you.
But it is those who maintain a steady pace
who will endure to the end.

Endurance is what you must have.
Those who sprint through the race of life,
may feel their faith and strength begin to weaken.
And those who fall behind,
may quickly lose sight of their vision to reach the end.
While those who maintain a steady pace win,
because they endured.

Implement an Action Cycle and Make the Decision to Follow Through

Any successful entrepreneur will tell you that success comes through taking consistent action, being persistent, and following through. That is why it is important to set reasonable timelines so that you won't fall behind, become frustrated or experience disappointment when you don't meet a specific goal. Of course, there's no guarantee that you will complete every goal that you set exactly on time. But if you adopt a habit of setting realistic timelines for completing goals and being consistent with your follow through, you will achieve success on a consistent basis. An action cycle consists of the following four factors:

Factor 1: Take Action. Begin acting on the first step. When one step or objective is completed, immediately move on to the next step.

Factor 2: Track Progress. Review what you have accomplished thus far to make sure you're on track.

Factor 3: Make Adjustments to Your Plan. As you proceed, if certain areas of your plan are not working to your satisfaction or as planned, modify the plan or find a different approach. You can also do the following:

- Find role models who are getting the results you want and learn how they get their results.

- Find a mentor, advisor, or coach who can offer you proven solutions to help you stay on track.

Factor 4: Take Action Again. After making adjustments, continue to move forward.

Narrow Your Niche and Find Your True Target

As a new business owner, you have to remember that you are now the accounting department, marketing department, sales department—you are everything. Sometimes it gets to be very overwhelming.

What I always tell my clients is, on your calendar—whether it's once a week, ten times a week, it doesn't matter—you have to put down marketing and put down sales, and make them appointments because you wouldn't stand up an appointment. Pretend it's a new client coming in—you'd never stand them up, so why would you risk not having the ability to reach clients or prospective clients to sell to them? You need to put that on your calendar.

If it means that you don't want to pick up the phone because it weighs 900 pounds, go out and do some networking and build relationships, because you have to be able to support this habit that you have and that habit is your business. How do you do that if you don't get in front of people, whether it's over the phone, on the computer or however you want to do it? If you don't have people to talk to, then you don't have business. If you don't have business, then there is no way for you to support yourself.

Who is your target market? Inevitably, people will give you this gigantic target. "My target is women." Well, what about women? We go through this process of the needs analysis. You might say "I want to work with boomer women." What about the boomer women? "I want to talk to the ones that are recently divorced, separated or widowed."

Every time you do that, your niche goes down. Now that you've become an expert in your field, not only can you find your people, but people can refer people to you because you're now the expert in that field. If you're new in business and you have to make some money, you've got to be able to narrow that niche and be able to offer something to your market.

— Judy Hoberman, President, *Selling in a Skirt*

The Essential Keys to Achieving Your Business Objectives Faster

Consistently promoting your business always is necessary for long-term success. Numerous methods can be applied to help you market and promote your company. As a new business owner or even a seasoned entrepreneur, networking can be one of the fastest methods for building and growing your company. Networking is the act of connecting with others in similar fields of interest, finding common ground, and learning how each person can serve and support the other.

A few ways to quickly jumpstart your business can include joining a Master Mind group, promoting yourself and your ideas to people in your community, and joining relevant live and online networking groups.

Start or Join a Mastermind Group

A mastermind group is an excellent way to stay focused on your business goals while discovering new ideas and gaining insights from others. Joining these groups will help you be accountable for achieving your objectives. A group might consist of school teachers, motivational speakers, SEO experts, small business owners, or others who have similar goals to each other.

Benefits of a Mastermind Group

Learn from peers. Since everyone in a mastermind group has a unique knowledge base and skill set, you're bound to learn something new.

Think bigger. Being exposed to other people who have achieved more than you will encourage you to reassess your goals. Perhaps your goals were previously a little too conservative or a little too small. Hearing success stories will help you realize just how much more is possible.

Access support. It isn't easy to pursue your vision alone, and a mastermind group can be a great source of encouragement and emotional support, as well as expert advice.

Expand your social circle. You'll find that you have much in common with the members of your mastermind group. What better way to widen your social circle than by starting or joining a mastermind group?

Be accountable. Since all the other group members will know your plans, they can help hold you responsible and ensure you follow through on them.

Network. Mastermind groups tend to be attended by people seeking new opportunities. If you're looking for funding, a business partner, or even something closer to home like shared childcare, then a group can be a great place to start.

Generate new ideas. When faced with a particular challenge, it is useful to seek a different perspective—or ten different views. A mastermind group can be a quick and effective way to generate novel solutions.

There are so many existing mastermind groups, whether online or in your local community, that you're likely to find one that suits your requirements. But even if you don't find one, you can always start one yourself.

Building a Mastermind Group

Here are some useful tips for getting a mastermind group started:

Look for diverse skillsets. It's best if everyone can contribute different expertise to the group. If your core topic, for example, is real estate investment, then ideally, you might find a developer, a builder, an agent, and a banker to be group members.

Reach out to potential members. Not only should they be able to contribute something useful to the group, but they should also be in a position to benefit from it themselves.

Choose the best candidates. Bigger isn't necessarily better for a mastermind group. Select excellent members who match your topic and objectives.

Establish a well-defined topic and objectives. If you want to attract the right members, then you'll need to be clear about exactly who you want to join. Are you starting a group about online marketing or product design, for example? What do you hope to achieve with it?

Make sure all members have similar levels of commitment. If commitment levels within the mastermind group are mismatched, with highly driven members on the one hand and hands-off members on the other, then discord is sure to grow while you accomplish very little.

Determine a meeting schedule and format. Be as clear as possible in the beginning so that everyone has the same expectations. Will you meet bi-weekly or monthly? How will each meeting proceed? Will a member act as chair, and if so, will it always be the same member? A lack of clarity around these details can waste a lot of time.

Make sure everyone contributes. High-functioning mastermind groups are characterized by a healthy exchange of ideas in which everyone benefits. There should be no free riders; but equally, less vocal members should be allowed the space to contribute.

Here is what you should do when you join a mastermind group:

- Get together with open, goal-oriented people who want to learn about your goals too.

- Listen to the opinions of other group members and give constructive advice yourself.

- Share with the group what you're planning to accomplish and when you hope to achieve it.

- Help members stay focused and motivated during meetings.

- Reach out to individual members to encourage them and hold them accountable.

- Meet at least once a month to discuss achievements and challenges and to generate new ideas and solutions for everyone.

If you want to learn more about mastermind groups, the best way to begin is simply by attending one or more meetings. You'll find that most groups are open to a prospective member listening in on a meeting.

Please don't rush to join: keep trying different groups until you find one that best suits your objectives. Be explicit about what it is you want to achieve. Don't settle for a partial fit—you'll only end up wasting everyone's time, including your own. Bear in mind that you may eventually need to start your own group.

Treat Negotiations Like a Game of Chess

Some people give in so quickly when they're attempting to negotiate a deal for different reasons. Number one, they fear not knowing what to do. Number two, they have not prepared succinctly enough to understand what it is that they want from the negotiations.

That's to say, if you're looking for $100,000, but you know you can live with $75,000, you have a bracket. You have a medium, in this case, let's say $100,000 to $75,000. Then throughout the negotiation, you get to $125,000, and the other negotiator is either beginning to become squeamish or gives you non-verbal signals that you're a little too close to the edge. If you keep pushing, you may lose the whole deal.

People not understanding where they are in the negotiation may be fearful to even attempt to negotiate. A lot of people don't like to negotiate. They feel as though it's going to make them look cheap. But as my mother said when I was a kid, "Wouldn't you rather have more of your money than somebody else?"

The answer to that is a definite yes. People need to become more aware of the negotiation process. There's a whole realm of steps that one goes through in order to perfect a very good and proper negotiation outcome. Most people do not know that and that's the reason why they're somewhat afraid to enter into negotiations.

To prepare for business negotiations, first of all, do your background gathering of information. Find out everything that you can about the target with whom you will be negotiating as soon as you possibly can. As an example, why are they negotiating? Why is it that they are negotiating with you? What other resources can they bring to bear on this situation that might allow them to have leverage? What resources do you have that you could use as leverage? What will the other individual do if they can't close the deal with you? How much time do they actually have to close the deal? Where else can they go to get additional assistance and time to save the deal? What happens if they can't get the deal? What happens if they don't have sufficient resources to get the deal? Who else can they align themselves with?

There is a conglomerate of questions that you need to ask yourself and be able to answer. After that, you want to map the course the negotiation may take and have alternative courses if you have to renew the negotiation. You also have to know how to get back on the path you need to be on in order to have a successful outcome. If you put all of those thoughts and plans together, you will act upon what you have to do, like a chess game, thinking three, four, five moves ahead. If they do X, and you thought they were going to do Y, you have a contingency plan in place to address X as opposed to Y. That's how you put your whole negotiation scenario together. That's how you become more successful with the outcome you're seeking.

— Greg Williams, CSP, The Master Negotiator
and Body Language Expert

Promote Yourself

Another effective way to achieve your goals faster is through self-promotion. Share your ideas with people who can help you accomplish your goals.

- Talk with coworkers, friends, family members, or business associates who can potentially help you pursue your goals.

- Network with new people who have similar interests or are in the same field.

- Ask for references.

- Seek mentors and advisors for encouragement, resources, and plans to help you succeed.

- Write to people you admire, tell them what your interests are, and ask them for helpful suggestions.

- Ask people in your field of interest if you can shadow them at work and take notes on how they accomplish their tasks.

- Seek a part-time position or volunteer in your field of interest.

The advantages of self-promotion include the following:

- Keep your name and your idea in the minds of important people who may have an interest in helping you or working with you in the future.

- Open doors to advanced opportunities.

- Learn about possible funding support.

- Create great contacts you can refer to in the future.

Join Networking Groups or Attend Networking Functions

Joining related networking groups both live and online will help you meet people who can assist you with accomplishing your vision. A great online business networking site is LinkedIn. This social network is solely devoted to entrepreneurs, business owners, corporate management, and professionals. LinkedIn has hundreds of individual groups you can join based on your interests. This site is perfect for helping you to reach your goals of increasing your finances, researching networking groups that are related to making passive income, creating small business opportunities, or exploring entrepreneurial pursuits.

Don't join regular social or dating groups if your focus is not to meet people socially. These groups may not be as effective and can consume much of your time—time which could otherwise be wisely devoted to achieving your specific goals. Get into the habit of attending networking functions every month that are relevant to your area of interest. This is an excellent way to meet people who you can connect with and build successful business relationships over time.

3 Things Small Businesses Need for Growth

If a small business has limited finances, in order to continue to grow, obviously three key things would be required: 1. You need to have a differentiated product. 2. You have to make sure you have an item that people want in the marketplace. 3. It's critical to understand who your consumer is, or your customer, and make sure that your product is something that they're looking for. That's just a critical step for any business.

I think the vision of your organization is important because you can develop a lot of items, but if you don't have a key focus on what you're trying to do with your business or your product line, it's easy to get distracted and just take whatever opportunities come up. So, I think having a strategic focus is really critical.

From a product standpoint in marketing, it's consumer insights, understanding what consumers are doing with our product, so that we can make a better product for them. I think that helps us to spend marketing dollars smartly because we have a better understanding of the type of marketing we should be doing. You can't just throw things against the wall and see if they stick. It's so expensive to launch items now, and it's expensive to market them. We try to do as much up-front research as we can before we start investing dollars in marketing.

As a company, we are involved in every step of the growing process—from grower to consumer, the entire process, which results in a higher-quality product.

If, for some reason, a business owner is unable to monitor their entire process, then to ensure their product is being created in a high-quality manner, they've got to have good systems in place. I think it's key if companies look at where their value proposition is along the supply chain.

It's critical because there are niches, even if you may not be doing what we do in taking it from the field to the shelf and controlling the process along the way. There are still very successful companies within our industry that don't have that same business model, but they're really experts and they're focused on one piece of that process. And that's where they can provide value.

You really need to understand what your value proposition is along that whole supply chain to make sure that it's differentiated, to ensure that you're not one of hundreds of companies that do the exact same thing, that you're providing something that's different.

— Jeffrey Sanfilippo, Chairman and Chief Executive Officer,
John B. Sanfilippo & Son, Inc., Fisher Nuts Brand

Section Three

Transform Your Business into a Recognizable Brand

Successfully Marketing Your Product with a Whisper

It is not true, usually, that it takes a while to gain market share. That's a fallacy. I've helped launch over 100 products or companies. One of the places where we have the largest amount of gravity is around how we launch our products or our companies into the market because we do it backward.

Let's say we have a product. It could be a company. It could be a service, but let's just say we have a new product. We develop this product. We keep it secret from our sales force and the market. We develop it and a week or two before it's going to come out or maybe a month, we begin to talk about it. A week before it comes out, we talk to the press. Then we put the press release out and train our sales reps and we have this big boom. Here it is, this big lightning bolt, "Here's our new product," with no one using it, no sales, no revenue. We're starting from that point in time and we have no credibility. That is not the way to become successful in a market launch.

Early on you want to say, "I'm going to take my product concept and go to the top ten target profiles who I think will buy this. And I'm going to test it. Then I'm going to go to them, and I'm going to have them begin using it, or I'm going to show it to them. I'm going to have them begin talking about it quietly." What you want to do is have customers using your product. You want to have a sales force out selling your product. You want to create a buzz in the market about it before you ever announce it.

I refer to it as whispering, but what you want to do is market and whisper because everybody wants to know about the thing that only a few people know about.

It sets you up for success. By the way, it's cheaper than the way we usually launch products. It's much more cost-effective, and it sets you up to be credible.

> — Rebel Brown, Business Consultant,
> Market & Product Strategist and Turnaround Expert

From Best Kept Secret to Industry Leader

Publicity: The Great Equalizer

The way to successfully develop your business into a recognizable brand is to position yourself as a leader by building influence, credibility, and authority in your field.

Small businesses become medium-sized businesses and medium-sized businesses become large companies by consistently staying in front of their target market through media opportunities and by sharing stories that reach their audience on an emotional level.

No matter how small or large a company may be, publicity or media exposure becomes the great equalizer. It allows every business owner, entrepreneur, and CEO to present themselves as experts and leaders in their industry and stand out from their competitors. All this requires is creating a strategy that is aligned with the needs of your audience.

Publicity is the fastest and most cost-effective way to build momentum and influence while gaining local, national, and even international attention for your business. While it can be tricky to navigate this field, which is saturated with well-meaning but ineffective or even damaging advice, mastering publicity—and media—can be the key to unlocking the next levels of success for your brand or business.

A key question to ask yourself while developing your brand is, "How do I want to be perceived?" When people see your business name or logo, what do you want them to think and how do you want them to feel?

Common Myths About Publicity

There are several myths about publicity that keep many entrepreneurs from getting the exposure they deserve. These myths often become roadblocks to their success and as a result, they miss extraordinary opportunities.

A small business owner faces numerous struggles in the beginning stages, from not having enough resources (time, money, support team) to finding the balance between maintaining a personal connection with your audience and scaling up. A small business is its own delicate ecosystem and in order to grow with long-lasting results, it's critical to have a smart publicity strategy that won't derail you.

Let's briefly explore and debunk some of those misconceptions that continue to prevail in the small business community.

Myth #1 - Any media exposure is good.

That's not exactly true. Gaining worthwhile coverage requires relevancy. The first question you need to ask yourself is: Are the media outlets I'm reaching out to aligned with my industry?

You should develop a solid intentional plan for the type of media outlets you're going to approach. Think about what value you want to bring to their audience.

If you want to achieve success in getting the right kind of publicity, target your approach by contacting the right media outlets. A one-size-fits-all approach is not recommended because your pitch must be aligned with what the journalist covers to increase your chances of getting the interview.

Myth #2 - The only media coverage that matters is at the national level.

You don't need to be featured in major publications or on major news or talk shows to significantly impact your business and your income. It might seem like you're thinking big but on the contrary, it's limited thinking and will keep you from getting the media exposure you deserve.

Getting great publicity doesn't mean you have to focus on getting national coverage. Local and regional coverage can often produce much better results because of the targeted audience and relevancy. When crafting your publicity strategy, your initial approach should be to reach out to local media first. Starting locally gives you the experience needed as you hone your interviewing skills and will help prepare you for much bigger opportunities, including national media exposure which will come later.

Myth #3 - I need to do a lot of interviews to see results.

That is one hundred percent incorrect. You don't need to do 1,000, 500, or even 50 interviews in order to reap huge benefits. The same amount of revenue potential lies within 10 interviews as it does in 100 or 1,000 interviews.

You must be strategic and creative in how you leverage your existing media coverage. It's about delivering quality rather than obtaining quantity. If you have the right audience, the right host, the right reporter, and the right message, that is going to build momentum.

Myth #4 - I need a publicist in order to get media coverage.

As a small business owner, you don't need to spend thousands of dollars to share your message with your target market while in the early stages of growth.

Until you reach the point where you absolutely can't, every business owner should do their own publicity. In the beginning, every detail matters in developing what will ultimately be your "image," and you don't want to hand that essential creation process to someone else.

Taking charge of your public image and controlling your own media strategy can feel intimidating at first, but at the end of the day, no one knows your business or your audience like you do.

In those few formative years when you're first building your public image, maintaining control of your publicity strategy is key. Not only that, it's imperative to continue prioritizing and nurturing your relationship with your target market.

Being in charge of your publicity also comes with some serious benefits that an outside person just can't touch.

How to Generate Positive Publicity for a New Business

It's essential that, whether as a new or existing business owner, you adjust your thinking from "How can I generate publicity fast?" to "How do I generate *positive* publicity that will *last*?"

Before you start posting on Instagram, scheduling interviews on local TV or running ads in the newspaper or magazines, you need to look inward. You need to build a solid foundation that can bear the weight of growth and success.

What's Your Why?

You need to know what your "why" is for your brand.

A lot of people in business talk about mission as your purpose, which is true. Understanding your mission means knowing what actions you want to take and the kind of impact you want to make. This isn't just something you write on the "About" page of your website. It's your roadmap to the business you're going to be building.

To bring clarity to your why, ask yourself:

- What is important about building this brand?

- What kind of difference do I hope to make?

What's Your How?

If you want to make any progress in your business, you need to think about the way you want to operate—how you want your brand to be perceived.

- When people think of your brand, what do you want them to imagine?

- Is your brand high-energy and youthful? Serious and reliable? Quirky and fun?

There's no wrong answer except no answer. Think about your audience and what they would respond to best.

What's Your Where?

- Where are your customers located?

- What media outlets do they watch?

- Where do they get their news?

- Do they use social media?

- Do they read blogs?

- When they need to find a new company or product, how do they decide who to purchase from?

It's important to know where your customers and clients already are so you can go to them instead of expecting them to seek you out.

Find out who the influencers are in your industry and connect with them. Once you're in touch with influencers who already have a huge base, learn from them.

- What kind of content do they produce?

- What problems do they solve?

- Why are they in the space they're in?

If you can answer these questions when talking to an influencer in your space, you'll have the basic ingredients to start building your audience. Speaking with and asking questions to an influencer to get a deeper understanding of your space and audience is priceless.

Important Components for Developing a Successful Media Strategy

Part of creating a media strategy means getting really clear on your business goals, vision, and mission, and knowing what messages you should be delivering to your target audience. It requires you to understand your market including the following:

- Who is your market?

- Why does what you offer matter to them?

- How will it change their lives?

Getting media exposure and building brand awareness is all about providing the media with valuable information that will help enlighten, educate, and inspire their audience to act.

Your target market or audience should be aligned with the media outlet's audience that you are reaching out to. You must provide information and insights that will help them improve their lives in some way.

When you consistently share a message that is interesting and attractive to a set group of people, that's when you grow a loyal audience and develop true brand awareness.

In your publicity strategy, you should be targeting the same audience over and over, in whatever spaces they occupy. When you show up consistently with the same message and delivery, you'll eventually be remembered—and being *remembered* is key.

Craft Messages That Stimulate Your Audience to Act

Publicity isn't just about getting on TV. It's about knowing what you want to say, who you're saying it to, and why you're saying it. It's about using the media intentionally to build an image.

A key message is a compelling statement about an issue on which your company or organization takes a stand.

It's imperative to develop key messages or sound bites for every product or service you offer in your business. They are the core messages you want your target audience to hear and remember long after you do the interview. When delivering your key message, you want everyone to understand the same basic thought behind the message.

A few elements to take into consideration:

- Answer the questions: Why should the audience care about what you have to say and why should they act on it?

- Key messages should be designed to achieve and support your company's main goals.

- Your key messages should create some type of motivation to do something.

Pitch the Media Your Best Newsworthy Story Ideas

Just as you would pitch your business to a potential investor to obtain funding, getting media exposure requires you to pitch reporters and journalists. Pitch them newsworthy story ideas that are of interest to their audience. This is part of the relationship-building process.

Do you know what makes you newsworthy?

The topics and story ideas you choose will play a huge role in the types of interviews you'll get—it's about being relevant and knowing what topics appeal to the media. You need to select topics that are always on the minds of people in your market and have the most impact on their lives.

There are a few questions you should ask yourself when developing newsworthy angles for the media, including:

- Do you want to warn your audience about something that could change their lives forever?

- Do you have information that contradicts what everyone else is talking about?

- Do you have information to share that addresses new trends in your industry?

Thinking about these types of things will help you create story ideas and media pitches that successfully attract the media to you and present extraordinary opportunities in your business.

Credibility, Authority, and Influence: You Can Have It All

Credibility, authority, and influence are the three cornerstones of any media strategy. If you can master all three, you'll be well on your way to booking whatever appearances you want, getting your pick of clients, and being a go-to expert in your field.

Credibility: Credibility is simply whether your audience believes what you say, and it's based on your reputation and track record.

One of the most effective ways to build credibility is through referrals, testimonials, and gatekeepers. When other credible people speak on your behalf, people are more inclined to believe you. However, once you lose credibility, it's difficult to regain it.

Authority: A thought leader is a person who helps to guide the trends of a specific field. Every single industry in existence is constantly growing and changing, and thought leaders are the people in front saying, "Let's explore this route to make things a little better for mankind."

You become an authority by being consistently credible. People must believe you to trust you enough to follow what you say. To be a thought leader, you need to contribute your own original thoughts and not simply restate what people already know.

Influence: Real influencers have the ability to inspire action and motivate changes in their audience's behavior.

To become an influencer, you need to be credible and have authority. And then, you need to give people a call to action. You can't motivate action if you aren't giving people specific actions to take.

A good media strategy will emphasize boosting all three: credibility, authority, and influence. So, before you begin seeking media exposure, ask yourself if you're prepared to give your audience a reason to believe you, if you can contribute original thoughts to your field, and if you can outline specific calls to action.

Increase the Impact of Your Marketing Through Storytelling

Humans have told each other stories for as long as they have walked the earth. Indeed, storytelling is one of the things that makes us unique. Oddly, the importance of this universal human impulse is often forgotten in business, in favor of objective information and metrics. However, storytelling is a better way to connect with customers on an emotional level, because emotions are typically what drives them to act. Through stories, you can communicate clearly and succinctly what your business is about, including the advantages of your product. Facts and figures are great, but there is no substitute for a compelling story if you are trying to attract customers or clients.

How do you share your brand with the world? How do you communicate what your business is about on a massive scale? And most importantly, how do you build a connection with your target audience in a meaningful way that moves them to action?

The secret is publicity. But, once you have their attention, what do you say?

It all comes down to *narrative*.

Any brand you've seen and loved—from your favorite go-to expert to ultra-successful mega-corporations—has these five key stories at their foundation, and successful business owners turn to them in every single media appearance or publicity opportunity.

1. Brand Story

This is the story of your brand or business. Think of it as your mission statement and a superhero origin story all in one. This story defines your brand image—internally and externally.

Usually, the founder will use a brand story to tell how the business came to be and highlight the business's values and culture.

Stories are very important for your brand because they contribute tremendously to your brand's image.

2. Personal Story

A personal story is, simply put, a story from someone's life. In general, personal stories give the audience insight into who you are as a person and are fantastic for sprinkling into speaking engagements or interviews.

Often, people use personal stories to share how they overcame obstacles to reach where they are today—sort of a point A to point B journey.

3. Product Story

Product stories are like personal stories in that they are stories about your product or service. They are extremely flexible, and the objective is to spark your audience's interest.

Often, product stories share how the product was developed, why it came into existence, the problem that inspired the product, or even how a customer used the product in a unique or creative way.

4. Customer Story

You may have heard customer stories framed as testimonials. These are one of the most powerful types of stories and are very similar to personal stories in that they are the personal stories of your customers.

The objective of customer stories is to convey authenticity, trustworthiness, and social proof to your audience. Customer stories must be genuine if you want them to be effective!

5. Employee Story

The fifth and final type of story all business owners should know is the employee story. Employee stories are engaging because they take your audience behind the scenes and add a human element to your company.

Through employee stories, your audience gets a glimpse into the inner workings of your company and discovers how every person involved makes a difference.

Why Storytelling Works

Storytelling is an important part of every business and it leads to increased conversions and sales, but why exactly does it work?

People don't like being sold to, but they love hearing stories.

Storytelling is an ethical method of something I call *covert selling*. It allows you to appeal to people's emotions and build a connection long before an offer is even on the table. It is a much more authentic way of connecting with a potential customer that shows you value them more as a customer than as just a sale.

People Don't Remember Statistics

Data has the power to influence people, but by itself, it won't inspire action. The crucial first step in generating momentum and results is to build a story around your company's vision that will capture people's imaginations.

Most of us don't remember statistics. Without context, numbers don't mean much. For numbers to influence your audience or impact the way they think, you need to ground the numbers in reality, which means developing a story around them.

Your story goes where facts, figures, and analysis cannot: into people's hearts. A distinguishing story about you or your brand is one of the most memorable ways to establish a connection and build a relatable persona.

People Are Driven by Emotions and Logic

No one is exclusively driven by logic or emotions. We all make decisions based on a combination of both. And while we may certainly differ on whether we tend to weigh emotions or logic more heavily, especially when it comes to purchasing decisions, both matter immensely.

Storytelling gives business owners and entrepreneurs a way to seamlessly integrate emotions and logic. Stories can present a cause and effect relationships that appeal to our desire for logic while displaying an internal transformation or success that appeals to our emotions. Storytelling, when done right, is a powerful tool for any company looking to make a positive impression.

Humans are naturally drawn to stories. For centuries, it's how we've passed down information, shared experiences, and made connections with other humans. When you apply that to the business world, storytelling becomes the bridge you build to connect with your audience, influence change, add value to your products or services, and even shape company culture.

When a business integrates smart storytelling into its strategy, it first and foremost attracts the right people. Using a tone of voice that is authentic to your industry and audience can immediately filter through the noise to reach your target demographic.

A story, no matter how great, will never be heard if it's not being told in a way that captures the attention of your market.

But if the right people do hear it? Strong storytelling can drive action forward and influence decisions. Stories are compelling because of the emotional factor.

To get started, think about the following questions:

- Why do you do the work you do?

- How do your values align with the work you do?

- What is the vision for your life?

- How does your life vision intersect with your work?

Open a notebook or journal and begin jotting down your thoughts and answers as you work through this process to uncover your brand story. Think about your vision and your experiences, and ask yourself why. Uncover the reasons for the decisions you made or the steps you took to start your business. Consider each major failure, success, change, realization, or experience that led to results and had an impact on what you're doing today.

Use the following points to get started with journaling:

Talk about the moment when you knew for certain that you needed to pursue the career or path that you have today.

Share an event or situation that was a key turning point or defining moment in your life.

Talk about a principle that you believe is fundamental to who you are and how you do what you do.

Talk about your influencers. Identify a time when a mentor, teacher or coach influenced you and how that contributed to who you are today.

Talk about an experience that helped to define the reason why you started your business or a new career.

Talk about unforgettable moments in your career or daily life that reinforced your principles or your perception of what you do.

Create the Right Story for the Right Audience

Every story you tell should be tailored to the specific audience you're targeting. For example, the story that you share with your business associates will be different than the one you tell your customers or your employees. For your business customers, you may choose a story that focuses more on the specifics of your life as an entrepreneur or business problems you solved. Your story for potential customers might be about the change you want to make in the world, a story to communicate your vision.

But there's one important thing that you need to remember: When it comes to storytelling, it's not the story itself that determines its effectiveness. There's a difference between the one you *want* to tell and the one you *need* to tell.

Your story needs to resonate with and affect your audience. There should be an emotional hook that evokes feelings of relatability and connection. So how can you make this happen? By selecting the right types of stories.

Develop Personas That Match Your Audience

The best way to choose the right story for the right audience is to create audience personas that will help narrow down your target market. While these personas may be fictional characters, they are based on real data and market research and one of the most useful tools for successful marketing.

You most likely have several different segments of people you want to reach, so the first step is to identify each type of audience and create a profile for that type of person.

Start by taking the time to research and understand your market's demographics. Where does each person live? How old are they? What kind of education and income level do they have? Create a solid foundation for each persona and then move onto the psychographics to fully build out that character.

Psychographics, which are the psychological attributes of your audience, include thoughts, feelings, opinions, values, attitudes, and interests. Figure out what challenges your audience members face, their interests, the kind of lifestyles they lead.

Attitudes and values, in particular, play a very important role in storytelling. If your story is in sync with those of your audience, it will resonate with them.

The more you understand your target audience on a detailed level, the more impactful your storytelling is going to be.

Best Practices for Storytelling

Emphasize Emotions: Identify the emotions that you want to trigger among members of your target audience and produce emotive copy that provokes sentiment. This will help people to connect with your story.

Align the Story with Your Brand: Ensure the story you present fits with your brand image and is consistent with how you want to be perceived.

Incorporate Conflict and Resolution: Regardless of the length of your story, ensure the plot that supports the story contains both conflict and resolution.

Present Relatable Characters: Present characters that are relatable to your target audience. They should be people your audience will understand, connect with, and support.

Be Authentic: Where possible, use real people and cases in your stories so that your audience will perceive them to be believable and trustworthy.

Show Rather Than Tell: The most effective stories show rather than tell. Don't present a story that simply tells the target market to buy your products or trust your services; show them the benefits they will access in a clear and relatable fashion.

Storytelling Mistakes to Avoid

The Stories You Want to Hear: Don't tell stories that are interesting to you. This isn't about you; it's about your audience. Focus on creating stories that are interesting to your audience and target market.

Faking It: Authenticity goes a long way in telling stories effectively. You want to establish trust and credibility with your stories; if you fake it, sooner or later you will get called out on it. Make your stories as real as possible, using real people and events whenever possible.

Promoting: The hard sell tactic doesn't work in storytelling so if products appear in a story, incorporate them subtly and tastefully.

Focus on telling the story and getting an emotional reaction first. This alone will translate to sales, no pushiness required.

A Weak Opening: You don't have to follow a chronological sequence when telling your story because sometimes, the best place to start isn't at the beginning. Instead, open strong by starting with a key moment that sets the scene, and then fill in the details around it.

No Emotion: A story without emotion will fall flat every single time. When you're able to trigger an emotion in your audience, that's what ultimately inspires them and drives them to act. Make sure your stories pack an emotional punch (use your audience personas to figure out what will resonate most with your target market).

Too Many Facts: You're telling a story, not doing a sales presentation. Since stories appeal to emotions, there's no need to include an excess of data or facts to make an impression. Too many statistics will get in the way of the storyline.

Research shows that likability is one of the main drivers behind consumer purchase decisions. While there are many ways to make yourself likeable, a good story about yourself or your brand is one of the most distinctive and memorable methods. Stories are memorable not only because of the emotional connection but also because they stand out.

You should use stories in your business and make sure they are on-brand. They need to be consistent with your brand image. The real subject of your story is the emotion it elicits in your audience—focus on that.

Identify, Connect, Click: How to Network Effectively

There are three steps in the relationship-building process. The first step is what I call the **identification step**, and this is where you identify people that you want to meet in life.

As part of this identification step, there is the step of meeting people by circumstance and happenstance. We meet people on elevators. We meet people in the mall. We meet people on airplanes. We meet people in workshops, seminars, and conferences. Identify and engage. When we engage a person, we exchange information or niceties perhaps. Ultimately, if we like what we feel and see, we exchange business cards or information. That's the first step in the process.

The second step in the process is the **connecting step**. Connecting is based on common ground. Common ground is based on people, places, and things. The more common ground you have with someone, the higher the trust level. The higher the trust, the more willingness a person has to share key concepts and information.

The third and final step is the **clicking step**. I wrote an entire book on clicking. Did you ever meet somebody, and you just clicked with them? When you click with someone, it simply means that you win, I win, and the people that we serve win. That's the end result of clicking.

Most people never get to the clicking step because they never reach the connecting step, which is following up, cultivating, nurturing, and building the relationship.

The other fatal flaw that people make when networking is that they network to get something. Wrong. You network to give and as you give, you get. If you aren't giving, you aren't getting.

You cannot take out of life that which you have not put into life, just as you cannot take out of the bank that which you have not put into the bank. That is the first and foremost principle of effective networking. You give first; you share always. The getting comes later.

— Dr. George C. Fraser, Chairman and CEO, FraserNet

Using Social Media to Grow Your Business

2.5 billion people actively use Facebook every month. YouTube gets over 2 billion visitors per month. One billion users are on Instagram. Over six hundred seventy million members are on LinkedIn. More than 330 million users are on Twitter, and over 300 million are on Pinterest. Those numbers continue to grow.

What is the significance of the number of users these social networks have? Succinctly, customers—whether they are existing or potential—your target audience is using a minimum of one social media platform.

Because these social networks receive a significant amount of traffic each day, they give you a way to engage with your target market. Social networks enable you to attract potential customers and interact with them. Without social media, you wouldn't have any other way to connect with such people.

Social media gives you the ability to reach customers, no matter where they are. Relying on customers within your vicinity is no longer the only choice you have. By engaging with people on social networks, you can turn your customer base from regional to international.

Your brand can be seen by a broad audience who may not be familiar with it. When you use social media consistently, you can develop a strong brand that separates you from the competition.

Social media gives you the ability to be seen as a resourceful authority in your industry. All you need to do is post new and insightful content regularly. However, to achieve this, you'll need to ask yourself a few questions:

- What platform should you be using?

- What approaches should be used to get noticed by the most significant amount of people?

- Will certain forms of content deliver better results than others?

- What is the best way to post content on a regular basis?

- Are there any etiquette rules that you should be following?

Some business owners mistakenly believe that they'll attract customers only by making an occasional post on a social network. Doing this will not deliver any results. You need a solid strategy to establish your brand on social media.

You should know what to post, where to post it, how frequently you will publish it, and other relevant aspects. It is vital to create a strategy if you want to interact with an audience. In short, you must put a plan together. The following steps can help you create a sound social network strategy.

First Step: Selecting a Suitable Platform

Your first step will be the most important one, and that is to select which platforms to focus on. Rather than attempting to leave posts on all social networks, concentrate on the ones that can impact your company.

To determine this, you'll need to understand a few things about your audience:

- On which social networks are they spending most of their time?

- Which social networks do they use to engage with businesses and brands?

- Which social networks influence them into making purchases?

- What platforms are the most successful influencers in your industry using?

If you have a relatively young audience, you should be using YouTube and Instagram, as their users are mostly millennials. If business professionals are who you want to focus on, then LinkedIn would be the better platform to use. If your target market is primarily women, Pinterest might be the best choice.

You should publish your content on the platform your target market spends the most time on. If you post content on platforms that your audience doesn't spend a lot of time on, your posts will receive minimal engagement.

If you aren't sure which platform your target market spends the most time on, don't be afraid to ask them.

Be sure to email people on your mailing list. Ask them directly which social networks they prefer using. You can create a poll on many social networks asking people this very question.

You can also find out where your target market spends the most time by looking at the stats for content you've posted. Check to see how many views your posts are getting per platform.

When determining which social network to use, factor in what your specialty is. Based on the services or products you offer, one particular platform may prove to be superior to the rest.

For instance, if you sell tangible goods, then visual platforms such as Pinterest and Instagram may be better suited for your brand. Conversely, if you offer services, then Twitter, LinkedIn, and Facebook may be more effective for you, as these platforms allow you to go into detail about your specialty.

When considering which social networks to use, think small instead of big. You'd be better off using one or two relevant platforms rather than continually posting on multiple platforms. Choose a suitable platform and post content to it regularly.

Second Step: Optimize Your Profile on Social Media

If you looked at a company's profile on social media and didn't see a logo, couldn't find a description about them, and saw that their posts were infrequent, would you feel confident giving them your business? Of course, you wouldn't.

Optimizing your profile on social media is essential. Your profile must be as attractive and informative as possible. To optimize your profile, keep the following recommendations in mind:

1. Your Username Should Be Professional.

The username you select should either be your company's name or your name. If you use a name like "RosePetals87," your brand won't come across as professional, which will diminish your odds of achieving success.

2. Your Profile Photo Should Be High Quality.

When uploading an image of either your logo or yourself, it should be of high quality, at least 300 dots per inch (DPI). Try to use a well-designed logo or a photo taken by a professional photographer.

The initial thing people will see when visiting your profile on social media is the photo you upload. That's why it's essential to leave them with a strong first impression, and that starts with a high-quality profile photo.

3. Your About Section Must Be Compelling.

In the About section, describe your business. The About section is where you explain what your company offers. Your description should be concise yet compelling.

Based on which social network you use, the amount of space you'll have to describe your offering or company may be limited. In such cases, explain why your company is different from the competition. What separates your offering from everybody else's? This is the type of information you need to tell people in the About portion of your profile.

Don't forget to add links to profiles on other social networks in this section as well as a link to your official website. The About portion of your profile should be as comprehensive as possible. People should be able to get a sense of what your company is about quickly and easily.

4. The Cover Photo You Upload Should Be Professional.

Cover photos can be uploaded to just about every social network. This photo will appear behind your profile photo. It should be a professional and high-quality image, just like the profile picture you upload.

If your company has a motto or slogan, think about adding it to the cover photo. Consider displaying imagery of a product you offer if you do not have a motto or slogan. The cover photo you select should emphasize something important about your company.

5. Add Contact Info.

Don't forget: You are using a social media platform to grow your company. As such, simplify the way potential customers can get in touch with you. In your profile's Contact section, add all the ways customers can reach out to you.

Your contact information may include your company's phone number, mailing address, email address, and other contact methods (Skype, Facebook Messenger, etc.). Also, encourage people to engage with you on a social platform directly.

Third Step: Schedule Your Posts

After your social network profile is optimized, you can map out the frequency of your posts and the content you want to post. This should be done before posting anything on social networks. Doing so can help you determine what specific content to post.

Some people use a calendar designated for social media content. This kind of calendar or schedule is an ideal way to decide what will be posted each day and when it will be viewed. Ask yourself the following questions when creating a social network calendar:

- How frequently do you plan to post? You should post once daily, at the very least. Followers will see that you are active on social networks.

- What kind of content do you intend to post? The type of business you run will define the kind of material to be shared.

- What formats do you plan to use? Companies that make the biggest impact use various formats when posting to social media. They post more than just text-based content. They use quizzes, polls, videos, photos, and images. The more media diversity you post, the more appealing you'll be to followers and potential customers.

Having a social network plan mapped out ahead of time can help you become more consistent when posting content.

Fourth Step: Begin Posting Content

After your content calendar is created, you can start posting things to social media. The content you post must contribute value if you wish to attract new clients while simultaneously satisfying current ones.

That's the most significant point here.

You are not posting for the sake of doing so. You are attempting to offer your audience information of great value. You are sharing information that can help people optimize their lives in some capacity.

Every post should benefit your audience in one way or another. The content you post should help audiences do the following:

- See something from a new perspective.

- Act if they haven't yet.

- Think positive, happy thoughts.

- Learn something interesting that they can apply to their lives.

You need to understand your audience in order to achieve success with your social media strategy. If you are familiar with your audience, you'll know what is valuable to them. Here are some examples of content worth posting:

- Inspirational quotes relevant to your niche

- Suggestions and recommendations on your subject matter

- How-to videos

- Live streams

- Motivational photos that inspire your target market

When your content calendar is created and you start posting on social networks, there is one question you should repeatedly ask yourself: **Will this contribute value to my target market?** If the answer is yes, then go ahead and post it. If the answer is no, refrain from doing so.

Fifth Step: Interact with People Who Follow You

You need to do more than just post something to your social media page. Social media's biggest strength is its ability to stimulate interactions between your followers and your company. Such interactions lead to more conversions.

You must interact with people consistently and regularly. All you need to do is answer questions, provide solutions to problems when you can, and respond to comments.

The effectiveness of social networks become apparent when a discussion is held between your company and the people who follow it. If you wish to establish relationships and increase your clientele using social media, then your conversations need to be authentic.

If you want more people to view your posts, it is crucial to interact with followers regularly. You should do the following:

- Communicate with your followers.

- Provide answers to their questions.

- Create engaging discussions.

- Solve problems when you can.

However, you shouldn't talk at your audience. Instead, you should endeavor to speak with them to create authentic connections. When having a discussion with people who follow you, consider these suggestions:

- Ask probing questions that will get them thinking about their business.

- Host live streams and provide a platform where people can talk to you directly.

- Conduct polls and surveys to learn more about them.

- Encourage people to provide feedback on certain subjects.

- Make a statement that encourages conversations. Always keep conversations positive, uplifting, and relevant.

Sixth Step: Follow Key People

Using social media entails more than simply growing your following. You also need to follow certain people and engage with them. Think about some of your industry's influencers and engage with the content they share. Leave sincere comments and share their posts, when applicable.

LinkedIn and Facebook have groups dedicated to every industry you can think of. One effective approach to engaging with industry peers is to become members of these groups. Take part in professional discussions and provide help to group members when you can.

Concentrate on contributing value instead of promoting your company. When you add value, you establish credibility and are seen as an industry expert.

As you engage in groups and follow other industry influencers, you will see that the information people share is valuable to others. What content resonates with you most? What posts have helped you in some way? What content gets the most responses? What type of content produces the most engagement and conversations? That is the type of content you should be sharing.

Seventh Step: Add Hashtags to Your Social Media Posts

Hashtags allow you to organize posts based on their subject. If you add a hashtag to something you post, it'll be categorized with other posts containing that same hashtag.

To use hashtags, all you need to do is add one to whatever you post. Hashtags come in this format: #hashtag or #keyword.

The hashtags you use should be relevant to the content you post. If you use irrelevant hashtags, you will diminish the impact of your social marketing. Unrelated hashtags annoy people and will be detrimental to your efforts.

Eighth Step: Experiment and Try Out New Things

As with other forms of marketing, using social media to promote your company means you'll need to consistently test to see what works. Social networks are always changing. To achieve success, you'll need to adapt to those changes.

By conducting tests, you'll find out what contributes the greatest value to those who follow you. From there, you can keep posting similar content. This will result in more engagement.

It's Time to Begin

The benefits of social media are tremendous. If you intend to use social media or are currently including it in your overall marketing strategy, implement the above steps to ensure you are getting the best results from your efforts. With social media you can do the following:

- Attract new customers and clients.

- Develop your brand into a recognizable name.

- Interact with new followers.

- Establish your company as an industry resource.

- Engage with industry influencers and build rewarding relationships.

- Learn more about your audience.

Section Four

Prepare Yourself to Declare Victory

The Two "F" Words to Eliminate from Your Life

I would ask people to eliminate their fear of failure. Individuals should ask themselves, "What would their lives be like if they could eliminate the fear of failure?" Life is not a dress rehearsal.

There are two words: fear and failure. Fear is just a mental construct; It's not the wind blowing or grass growing. So, if it's just a mental construct, you can eliminate it, because it doesn't exist.

The second word is failure. I submit there's no such thing as failure. You know there are experiences where the outcome is an issue of life, but you've gained from it, you've learned from it. If you sit and wallow over something that didn't go the way you wanted it to go, then you're wasting your life. It would be like driving a car by looking in the rearview mirror. You know you don't want to live your life like that, so why would you build your business like that?

In conclusion, I think people should eliminate the fear of failure and recognize that they need to be a person of action and live every moment to its fullest extent. Enjoy life, have some fun but stay focused on your business activities. If you're going to do things and build things, build them green, make them sustainable, because we all need to make our contributions to the planet by doing things that are right and energy efficient.

— Michael V. Roberts, JD,
Chairman and CEO, The Roberts Companies,
Author of *Action Has No Season*

Overcoming Challenges

In order to achieve your purpose, you must be willing to positively deal with and overcome the challenges of daily life. There is no success without hardship. Challenges will come in many different forms. For example, you may not have enough money, time, or support to do what you need to do. There may be times when you will find yourself at a crossroads and you are not sure in which direction to turn.

Don't spend a lot of time worrying about your problems. Instead create a plan to work through them. We know that worrying can make a problem seem much larger than it really is. You will either overcome your circumstances or they will overcome you. Having a strong foundation of faith, thinking positively, and reaching out to others is absolutely necessary to begin the process of overcoming all of life's adversities.

Often when we are faced with a challenge, we only see the big picture. We panic at the thought of having to deal with challenges. We lose confidence in ourselves and our ability to handle adversity. As a result, we push aside our problems and hope that they will resolve themselves.

Procrastinators may often refuse to acknowledge their problems, or they believe they are not important enough to deal with right now. There's never a better time than right now to begin creating a strategy for overcoming your business and personal challenges, especially when they affect your business and the people who are connected to it.

> *The person who makes a success of living*
> *is the one who sees his goal steadily*
> *and aims for it unswervingly.*
> *That is dedication.* — Cecil B. De Mille

Your quality of life and business success depends on how you deal with life's adversities and challenges. Sometimes setbacks are warning signs that changes may need to occur in our lives. View your challenges from a positive perspective and prepare yourself to overcome them. Here are some suggestions on beginning the process.

Realize that setbacks and challenges are inevitable.

Challenges are inevitable for every business owner, entrepreneur, CEO, and executive. Everyone who is successful at his or her business must create a plan to successfully deal with challenges. Some strategies include the following:

Recognize that no one succeeds at everything the first time, the second time, or even the third time.

Understand that one setback is not the end of the world. There are many other opportunities to succeed.

Anticipate that things will change when you maintain a positive attitude and create a plan.

Develop a plan to push forward with your ambitions.

Rethink your problem-solving strategy as needed.

Develop a plan to ensure that your business plan is complete.

Incomplete business goals can often be due to one or more of the following:

Restrictions or limitations you put on yourself.

Mistakes that you or other individuals connected to your business make.

Unexpected circumstances that occur while you are building your business or even in your personal life.

Not being physically prepared to take on the responsibility of running a business.

Lacking confidence about your ability to achieve your business goals.

Not planning your business goals strategically or thoroughly.

Not having resources available to you that are appropriate.

Not having enough education or knowledge in the area of your interest.

Not having enough support from others.

Each time you fail to face life's challenges, you have chosen to accept defeat. – Monica Davis

Set up a strategy for conquering your challenges.

Here are some ideas on how you can defeat challenges that you will encounter as an entrepreneur:

- View challenges as opportunities to overcome future obstacles.

- Immediately focus more on how to overcome the challenge and get the results you want to achieve.

- Look at solutions to challenges as a benefit. The longer you put off resolving the challenge, the worse things will become. Smaller problems can quickly become bigger problems simply because we did not correct them in a timely manner.

- As you solve problems, make note of the solutions. They may give you ideas or become solutions for future challenges.

Effectively approach your business challenges.

Now you can begin to consider effective ways to eliminate the problem, such as…

- Immediately plan your strategy for overcoming the problem

- Analyze and break the problem into smaller, manageable parts and identifying the underlying cause

- Ask how you can utilize the current situation to your advantage. How can you create a positive outcome?

- Learning from the experiences of other business owners (i.e., Don't be afraid or embarrassed to ask them how they overcame their business challenges).

- Consult your role models and pay attention to how they resolve their challenges.

- Constantly ask questions of qualified experts.

- Take pride in your ability to resolve problems. For example, look at what you've done in the past to keep your business running.

- Believe and trust that you can overcome it.

Analyze the reasons for the problem.

- Identify the overall challenge.

- Make note of each reason why you know or believe the problem exists. For example, if you're not fulfilling your customers' requests on time, it could be due to unproductive or undertrained employees, lack of materials, or any combination of those reasons.

- Identify options for how to fix or eliminate the cause of the problem. For example, you could have roundtable discussions with your team, outside experts, or a business coach to determine the best approach. Once you identify the cause, it becomes easier to eliminate the problem and to avoid it in the future.

- If similar setbacks are occurring often in other areas of the business, develop a list of reasons why.

Develop an action plan for overcoming your challenges.

Those strategies could include the following steps:

- Look for different ways to resolve your issue. Ask "What If" questions.

- Don't be judgmental when defining possible solutions. Outline all possible solutions in the beginning.

- Write down the actions you would take for each solution to resolve it.

- Rethink your strategy. Review your list of possible solutions to be sure you're not creating additional obstacles.

- Analyze each possible solution to determine the most effective approach.

- Always create an alternate plan.

- Determine what resources you need by asking the following questions…

A. People

- Who will I need to help me overcome the challenge?

- What role(s) will they play?

- Should I hire an expert or business coach to help me resolve the problem?

- How much time will they be expected to devote to helping me fix the problem?

- Can I resolve the problem myself?

- If so, can I afford to sacrifice time that ordinarily would be devoted to running my business?

- How will this business challenge affect my employees, partners, or members of my family?

B. Time

- How much time will be needed to resolve the entire problem?

- Will it interrupt the flow of business?

- If so, can someone else take care of the problem while I continue running the business or vice versa?

- Will this approach require additional money?

C. Materials

- What resources will I need to help me fix the problem?

- How will I obtain them and from whom?

- How long will it take to get them?

D. Money

- Will I need additional funds outside of my original budget to resolve the problem?

- If so, can I borrow the money?

- If I already have cash on hand…

  Will I leave another area of my life vulnerable if an emergency happens?

  What will be the long-term effects of using my emergency money now?

  When will I be able to restore these funds?

- Can I possibly barter with a business associate or an expert who is experienced in resolving such problems?

Once you have identified the problem itself, explored possible solutions, and decided on the best approach, it's now time to **take action** and execute your strategy. Notice the results you're getting. If the first solution is not working, execute the next one.

Getting Out of Your Head and into Greatness

To achieve success, number one, you have to continuously maintain a regimen to retrain your thinking, create new synapses to expand your vision beyond mental conditioning and circumstances.

Two, you have to constantly raise the bar for yourself and set goals beyond your comfort zone. In order to do something, you've never done, you've got to become someone you've never been.

Three, you've got to look at your relationships and upgrade them continuously. You must ask yourself, "What is this relationship doing to me?" There's a term in psychiatry called *relational illness*. Most people never achieve their goals because they have too many toxic, negative, energy-draining people in their lives. So, you have to look at your relationships and practice the principle of let go or be dragged. There are some people you need to let go; otherwise, they will drag you down.

The fourth thing that's important is to put your money where your mouth is. Once you open your mouth, you tell the world who you are.

When you incorporate these four actions along with effective communication skills, you upgrade your relationships, set goals beyond your comfort zone, and constantly are working to transform your mind.

"Be ye not conformed to this world; be transformed by the renewing of your mind." That for me is a recipe for getting out of your head, getting into your greatness, and living an extraordinary life.

— Les Brown, World-Renowned Motivational Speaker

Section Five

Blueprints

A Blueprint for Creating a Successful Business

1. List Your Goal ...

2. Analyze Your Goal by Answering the Following Questions ...

Why do I want to achieve this goal?

What products or services will I provide?

Who are my competitors?

Have I done the research to determine if what I'm offering is different than my competitors? What's unique about it?

How will my customers or clients benefit from the products
or services that I offer?

Why am I committed to starting the business?

How will creating the business affect my life in the short and
long term?

How do I plan to use this business goal to further enhance my
personal and professional life?

What will happen if I don't achieve my goal? How will I feel?

Will the results be worth my efforts? How?

Does my family or spouse support my decision to start a
business?

After I've accomplished my goal, what will I do next? What's my plan?

Do I plan to make the business a full-time endeavor? If not, will it just be a hobby or a part-time opportunity?

Will I remain a sole proprietor or will I bring on employees and partners?

If my company has not been started yet, have I researched and considered the pros and cons of different business structures (e.g., sole proprietorship, LLC, C corporation, and S corporation)?

Skills

Do I need special skills to run the business?

What current skills do I already have that can be applied to the business?

Do need to further develop my existing skills before starting my business?

What additional skills do I need? How much will it cost?

How long will it take to develop these additional skills?

Where will I obtain these additional skills?

How will I pay for the skills needed? Where will the funds come from?

Education

If required, do I have the appropriate education or degree to run the business?

If not, what type of education is needed?

What is the time frame in which I should complete the course(s) based on the time I set for achieving my business goals?

How will I pay for the education?

Where will I obtain the education?

How far will I have to travel (e.g., daily, weekly, or monthly)?

How will travel affect my time, my family's time, or other responsibilities that I have?

Time

Overall, how much time will I need to achieve my business or professional goal (e.g., daily, weekly, or monthly)?

Am I willing to commit the time and energy consistently?

Can I achieve the goal at a pace conducive to my current lifestyle? Or should I change my lifestyle to accommodate my business?

Should I set aside another project and make my business goal a higher priority?

Can I work on this goal in addition to other priorities of the same level or higher that must be met?

How will achieving this goal affect my time, my family's time, or other priorities?

Should I quit my job to pursue my entrepreneurial dream?

Can I financially afford to quit my job now? Do I want to take a high risk and quit anyway?

Can I continue working at my regular job and run the business at the same time?

How long should I work for my employer and pursue my business goals before deciding to resign? What factors should I consider?

Will simultaneously focusing on the business diminish the quantity and quality of my productivity at work?

Can I adjust my work schedule so that I can spend time on the business?

Materials

What materials or equipment are needed? How much will be needed?

How often will I need to purchase materials?

How much will the necessary materials cost?

Can I barter or trade with another company if I don't have the funds to purchase the materials?

What sources or vendors will provide the necessary materials?

Where are the vendors located?

Where will the money come from to purchase the materials? Will I have to borrow money?

What special software applications do I need to run the business?

Do I already know how to use them efficiently enough to get the job done in a timely manner? If not, how much time will I take to learn them?

Will I need to hire experts to handle specific work that requires special skills for such applications?

What type of business insurance coverage, if any, do I need for my type of business?

People

What other individuals might be affected during and after I accomplish my business goals?

How will they be affected in the short and long term?

What individuals can I use as mentors, leaders, and motivators to help me stay on course?

Who will I need to help me accomplish my goal?

Where are these people or groups located? How will I find them?

When are they available? What are their fees? How much time are they willing to commit?

If I cannot pay them, what will they expect from me in return? What am I willing to offer in return?

If I don't have enough money to implement major tasks, should I put the business on hold?

If I put the business on hold, how will that affect my overall plan or dream?

Should I ask friends, associates, or family members to help me implement those tasks for free?

What will they expect in return if I don't pay them for their time and effort?

How long will I need them to work for free before I am able to hire the right people to do the job?

What type of work ethic do they possess?

Although they are working for free, will they deliver work on time?

Will they consider my work a higher priority than some of their own obligations?

Do they have the relevant skills or experience necessary to do the work?

Are they 100% committed to helping me?

Should I do most of the work myself if I don't have the funds?

Will I have the time to perform every task until I hire qualified people?

How will doing everything myself affect the business, my personal life, and other obligations?

When can I bring on part-time or full-time employees?

If it is my intention to hire employees, do I have the proper structure in place for hiring employees?

If not, will I hire someone else to handle the task? What is the estimated cost?

Have I selected an attorney to assist with employee and other legal issues that might arise?

Have I selected an accountant to assist with payroll, other
accounting procedures, and taxes? If not, will I handle the
accounting process myself?

What type of health insurance benefits will I provide part-
time and full-time employees (e.g., health, vision, dental)?

Have I identified and written down all repeatable processes of
the business?

Will I hire an intern? What colleges or universities are
nearby that have excellent intern programs?

How much time do I anticipate for training the intern?

What roles or position will the intern fill?

Should I hire a virtual assistant for my administrative tasks?
What is their rate?

What type of people will I network with to encourage
business growth, possible partnerships, and joint ventures?

What types of organizations should I join that are related to
my business?

Potential Problems

What difficult challenges or obstacles might I have to
overcome while working on my business goal?

What resources might I need to overcome the challenge?

People

What type of people will I need?

How long might I need them to assist me in resolving my
business problem?

How much will I have to pay them and how often?

Money

How much will it cost to fix the problem?

Can I afford to push the problem aside if I don't have the money right now?

How will that decision affect the business, its employees, partners, and support team?

Can I use funds that were originally allocated to another part of the business to solve the problem?

Will fixing the problem now reduce the budget allocated for paying employees or other people who support the business?

If so, what can I do to quickly replenish those funds?

Time

Approximately how long will it take to resolve the challenge?

Am I willing to do what it takes to resolve the problem?

How will the time devoted to resolving the problem affect other individuals including employees, family members, and business partners?

Will fixing the problem require employees or business partners to devote personal time or extra work time?

Will they be willing to take time away from their personal lives to help me?

Marketing

Who is my target market or customer?

What is the demographic make-up of my audience?

Where are they located?

How will I reach them?

How will they purchase my product or service?

How often will I reach them?

Do they need or want my product or service?

How much money do I plan to spend on marketing both in the short term and long term?

How will I fund the marketing efforts to support my business?

What kind of image or brand do I want to create?

Advertising

How do I plan to attract customers?

What will be my message?

How will I say it?

What type of media will I use to deliver my message?

How much money do I need to spend on advertising?

Are there other ways of delivering my message that may be more cost effective?

Budget

What accounting system do I need to set up for the business?

How much money will I need to run the business?

What is my three- and five-year plan for the business?

What are all possible sources for funding the business for the short and long term?

Will I use my 401K to fund the business in its early stages? How will this affect my individual finances?

When do I estimate replenishing the funds?

If I'm still working, will repayment be automatically withdrawn from my paycheck?

Will I have to pay any penalties?

How long will it take to get the funds?

If I accept funding from others, will I have to repay the money? If so, how much, how often, to whom, and for what purposes?

What if I spend more funds than anticipated? Where will the additional money come from to keep the business running smoothly?

Do I have enough money set aside for emergencies?

At what point do I estimate paying myself a salary?

Do I need to open a separate business banking account?

What are the requirements for my state?

Will I need to open a business credit card account or more than one credit card account? How will this affect my overall credit if I already have personal credit cards?

Are any of my personal credit cards over the limit?

What is my debt-to-income ratio?

Do I anticipate any credit requests being denied? How will they affect my overall credit rating?

Have I searched for the best interest rates?

Will I be able to consistently make payments to avoid late fees and increased interest rates?

Do I qualify for any grants or other types of funding?

Return on Investment (ROI)

What results am I looking to obtain? How will I feel after I have achieved all my goals or met certain milestones?

Do I want the end results to be financial, material, emotional, or all the above? (For example, list how much money you want to gain through the business or other specific results.)

What creative ideas can I develop for new products or services to continue to increase my income and my return on investment?

Am I happy with my return on investment so far?

If not, what is keeping me from achieving a higher level of return?

What area of the business do I need to change to achieve maximum results?

3. Create an Action Plan ...

Act on your goal. Track your progress by reviewing your action plan to determine if you're on target. Remember to adjust as necessary. When one step has been completed, don't hesitate to move on to the next objective.

Short-Term Goals (1 to 5 months)

Action Steps/Objectives   Start Date   Proposed End Date   Completed Date

1. _______________________ _________ ________________ ______________

2. _______________________ _________ ________________ ______________

3. _______________________ _________ ________________ ______________

4. _______________________ _________ ________________ ______________

5. _______________________ _________ ________________ ______________

6. _______________________ _________ ________________ ______________

7. _______________________ _________ ________________ ______________

8. _______________________ _________ ________________ ______________

Mid-Term Goals (6 to 12 months)

<u>Action Steps/Objectives</u>   <u>Start Date</u> <u>Proposed End Date</u> <u>Completed Date</u>

1. _______________________ _________ ________________ _____________

2. _______________________ _________ ________________ _____________

3. _______________________ _________ ________________ _____________

4. _______________________ _________ ________________ _____________

5. _______________________ _________ ________________ _____________

6. _______________________ _________ ________________ _____________

7. _______________________ _________ ________________ _____________

8. _______________________ _________ ________________ _____________

Long-Term Goals (2 to 5 years)

<u>Action Steps/Objectives</u>   <u>Start Date</u> <u>Proposed End Date</u> <u>Completed Date</u>

1. _______________________ _________ ________________ _____________

2. _______________________ _________ ________________ _____________

3. _______________________ _________ ________________ _____________

4. _______________________ _________ ________________ _____________

5. _______________________ _________ ________________ _____________

6. _______________________ _________ ________________ _____________

7. _______________________ _________ ________________ _____________

8. _______________________ _________ ________________ _____________

A Blueprint for Overcoming Life's Challenges

You can download *A Blueprint for Overcoming Life's Challenges* at https://www.secretstosuccessbooks.com/success-blueprints-2.

1. Identify the overall challenge.

2. Identify specific reasons or causes why the challenge exists.

3. Determine what actions are needed to resolve the challenge. Create a strategy.

4. People

A. Whom will I need to help me overcome this challenge?

B. What role(s) will these people play in assisting me?

C. How much time will they need to help me correct the problem?

D. Can I resolve the problem by myself? If so, can I afford to take time away from running the business to fix the problem?

E. How will this business challenge affect my employees, partners, my family members, or others who are close to me?

5. Time

A. How much time will I need to resolve the problem?

B. Will taking time to solve this problem interrupt the flow of business or the entire business operation?

C. If so, can someone else resolve the problem while I continue to run the business or vice versa? If so, who? Will this approach require additional money?

6. Materials

A. What resources or materials will I need to eliminate the problem?

B. How and from whom will I obtain these resources?

C. How long will it take to get the materials?

7. Money

A. Will I need additional funds outside of my original budget to resolve the problem?

B. If additional funds are required, can I borrow the money?

C. Do I already have the required cash on hand?

D. If I must use my own funds, will another area of my life become financially vulnerable?

E. What will be the long-term effects of using my own funds now?

F. Will I be able to replenish the money later?

G. Can I barter with a business associate or an expert who is experienced in resolving such problems? If so, what can I offer them in return?

Once you have analyzed your business problem and determined how you will approach it, begin executing your strategy. Remember that you may have to adjust your action steps as you proceed.

A Blueprint for Using Mentors, Advisors, and Coaches

One of things that helped me quickly build a successful media company was the priceless advice of mentors, advisors, and coaches. Such people help you stay on target. Utilizing one or a combination of all three can help you stay focused and provide you with a wealth of information, guidance, resources, and tools to help you achieve maximum results in less time.

Mentors, advisors, and coaches help you to become accountable for your goals and actions. Many of America's top CEOs, billionaires, and entrepreneurs use coaches and mentors as a source of inspiration, knowledge, and ideas to help them expand their business and professional lives. Here are definitions of each professional and how he or she can help you achieve your goals.

Mentor

Mentors help foster an individual's personal and professional growth by sharing their knowledge and insights based on what they have learned over the years.

Advisor

Advisors are experts who offer official or professional advice in a specific area. They provide counsel or make recommendations about specific situations or circumstances.

Coach

Coaches help to facilitate ongoing growth within a specific area, such as your career, business, relationships, or various life goals. A professional coach supports you through the growth process by providing tools, resources, and advice on how to grow.

Mentors, advisors, and coaches can help you make sound and smart decisions for improving your business, professional, and personal life. Many of these experts are extraordinarily qualified to provide advice and unlimited support in the following areas:

- Financing, investments, and loans

- Sales and marketing

- Branding

- Public relations

- Personnel

- Leadership

- Business growth

For individuals who want to work on their personal or career goals, mentors, advisors, and coaches can also help you to improve in the following areas:

- Family and relationships

- Careers and employment

As you plan and implement your business and professional goals and further your ambitions, seek the advice of professionals. They will help you achieve maximum results and meet your objectives much faster than doing it alone.

Important Information for Purchasers of This Book

As you start your business, you must take time to map out a plan that will help you build a good foundation. That means answering important questions and addressing key business issues early on to help ensure long-term success. The blueprints provided in this book are also available online in PDF format. To access them, visit https://www.secretstosuccessbooks.com/success-blueprints-2.

Additionally, this book can be purchased in bulk. If you or your business associates hold special events where you engage with entrepreneurs or small business owners throughout the year, *Start Your Business Right* would make an excellent gift.

Here are a few ideas on how *Start Your Business Right* could be offered to provide value to your market:

1. If you sell products to entrepreneurs and small business owners, host Small Business Saturday events, where they register for a one-hour workshop held in your store. The attendees could receive a free copy of *Start Your Business Right* for taking the workshop.

2. If you are a restaurant or coffee shop owner and want to bring more business people into your establishment, offer a special menu on a given day or promote an event throughout the week where the first 50 business owners or entrepreneurs that order from your lunch menu will receive a free copy of *Start Your Business Right*.

3. For a non-profit or for-profit association that serves the small business community, a great way to offer more value for your membership would be to give them a free copy of the book.

These are just a few ways you can use *Start Your Business Right* to bring added value to your customers, clients, or members. Not only that, but you will also be strengthening networks of local businesses and encouraging the support of each other, something that all small business owners and entrepreneurs can benefit from.

If you're interested in a bulk purchase of this book or you have relationships with others who could benefit from bulk purchases, contact Monica Davis at monica@secretstosuccessbooks.com.

Opportunities for Business Growth

Media Mastery

It can be hard when you're just getting started in your business or when you have a limited budget, and yet you know you need to quickly get in front of your audience.

Most successful business leaders and influencers have one thing in common. What sets them apart is their ability to spot opportunities in the media and use those to showcase their expertise. Successful business leaders use the media to present themselves as authorities with something to offer—and to stay in the minds of their audience.

It's critical that you get as much exposure for your business as possible without spending an enormous amount of time or money to do it. Publicity offers you a level of endorsement that no other form of marketing can. When you are endorsed by the media, it opens unlimited opportunities and gives you instant credibility. It positions you as an authority in your field and gives you much more leverage.

The **Media Mastery** program is a step-by-step comprehensive virtual learning program. It provides easy-to-implement formulas and specific strategies you can immediately put to work to get your name in front of your prospects with little or no cash outlay by harnessing the potency of the media.

If you want to learn exactly how to put the media to work for you day in and day out, without having to spend a dime on ads, you'll want to invest in this course.

If you want to go from Best Kept Secret to Industry Leader, visit https://training.exceptionalmediacoaching.com to learn more.

Increase Your Influence and Profits with Your Compelling Story

Is your brand's narrative pulling its weight?

Today's most powerful marketing revolves around a relatable, meaningful brand narrative. That's because buying decisions and customer loyalty are deeply influenced by the way you position your company's purpose and vision. People don't simply buy products or services; they buy into the principles, values, and the story behind your brand.

A well-developed brand narrative can separate and elevate you from your competitors as well as connect you with your ideal audience.

Your story goes where facts, figures, and analysis cannot: into people's hearts. A distinguishing story about you or your brand is one of the most memorable ways to establish connection and build a relatable persona.

Are you using your story to its fullest potential? We can help you transform your brand by crafting a provocative narrative. Your authentic narrative has the power to impact millions.

To learn more about Monica's done for you program, **Increase Influence and Profits with Your Compelling Story**, visit https://exceptionalmediacoaching.com/your-story-equals-more-customers.

About the Author

Monica Davis is a business mentor, the founder of *Exceptional People Magazine*, an award-winning TV producer and host, media coach, and master communicator with over 21 years of experience in the media industry. She's helped hundreds of professionals, entrepreneurs, and CEOs advance their mission and vision through powerful and unforgettable brand narratives.

Her company, Atela Productions, is the recipient of eight 2019-2020 International Hermes Awards and has been named among industry-leading brands such as AARP, Deloitte, Hilton, IBM, Pepsi, and Fidelity Investments for conceiving, designing, and implementing innovative ways to brand, communicate, and market. She is also the author of *Welcome to the Top: Secrets to Success from Leading Entrepreneurs*.

Davis is available for coaching, training, webinars, and other online events. To learn more about these opportunities or to let her know about your interest in doing an event, contact Davis at http://www.exceptionalmediacoaching.com/contact.

A Message from the Author

I would love to hear from you.

As you begin your journey of becoming a new business owner or continue to pursue your current entrepreneurial path, I hope the information I've provided serves you well.

If you have any questions, insights, innovations, discoveries, or stories you'd like to share with me, please email me at monica@secretstosuccessbooks.com. You can also write to me at Atela Productions, 2961-A Hunter Mill Rd., PMB 624, Oakton, VA, 22124. Any stories submitted may be used in future publications, though names may be changed to protect privacy. Due to the number of inquiries we receive, notification of receipt may not be possible.

I encourage you to stay focused on your dream. Don't limit your thinking, and don't allow the negative opinions of others to define you. Be willing to step out of your comfort zone. Those who look well beyond the horizon, have faith, and consistently take action always encounter extraordinary opportunities.

You don't have to know every single step in the process to begin. All you need is a solid foundation on which to build your masterpiece.

Thank you for purchasing this book, and I wish you much success in your entrepreneurial endeavors.

With every wish for great achievements,

Monica Davis

703-273-2035

monica@secretstosuccessbooks.com

Your Action List . . .

Your Action List . . .

147

CPSIA information can be obtained
at www.ICGtesting.com
Printed in the USA
FSHW011030220920
73971FS